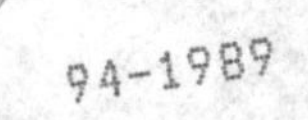
94-1989

P9-DVC-695

PARTNERING WITH EMPLOYEES

PARTNERING WITH EMPLOYEES

A Practical System for Building Empowered Relationships

DUKE NIELSEN

Jossey-Bass Publishers · San Francisco

Substantial discounts on bulk quantities of Jossey-Bass books are available to corporations, professional associations, and other organizations. For details and discount information, contact the special sales department at Jossey-Bass Inc., Publishers. (415) 433-1740; Fax (415) 433-0499.

For sales outside the United States, contact Maxwell Macmillan International Publishing Group, 866 Third Avenue, New York, New York 10022.

Manufactured in the United States of America

The paper used in this book is acid-free and meets the State of California requirements for recycled paper (50 percent recycled waste, including 10 percent postconsumer waste), which are the strictest guidelines for recycled paper currently in use in the United States.

The paper used in this book is acid-free and meets the guidelines for permanence and durability of the Committee on Production Guidelines for Book Longevity of the Council on Library Resources.

The ink in this book is either soy- or vegetable-based and during the printing process emits fewer than half the volatile organic compounds (VOCs) emitted by petroleum-based ink.

Library of Congress Cataloging-in-Publication Data

Nielsen, Duke, date.
Partnering with employees : a practical system for building empowered relationships / by Duke Nielsen.
p. cm.—(The Jossey-Bass management series)
Includes bibliographical references and index.
ISBN 1-55542-565-8
1. Supervision of employees. 2. Quality of work life. 3. Interpersonal relations. 4. Job satisfaction. I. Title. II. Series.
HF5549.12.N53 1993
658.3'02—dc20 93-3775
CIP

FIRST EDITION
HB Printing 10 9 8 7 6 5 4 3 2 1 *Code 9359*

The Jossey-Bass

MANAGEMENT SERIES

CONTENTS

Part Two: Partnering in Action

PREFACE

Adversarial relationships between supervisors and employees can exist in any organization. These stressful transactions exact a high cost in productivity and quality. Furthermore, problems between supervisors and employees are at the root of many organizational relationship problems. The contentious and litigious nature of many relationships between organizations has inspired a management movement to create partnering between organizations. Organizations accomplish partnering through negotiated cooperation agreements that eliminate win-lose transactions. *Partnering with Employees* recommends applying a similar process to relationships between supervisors and employees.

As director of education and training for Associated General Contractors of Colorado from 1972 to 1987, I crusaded for win-win relationships between supervisors and employees, and I developed, published, marketed, and conducted leadership and supervision training sessions. The participants' positive reaction to my training materials was gratifying, but my subsequent research on what participants actually implemented from their training proved that they made little practical use of what they had learned. The reasons adversarial relationships between supervisors and employees continue to exist and the alternatives to those relationships are the focus of this book. *Partnering with Employees* offers an innovative, comprehensive, and widely applicable approach to supervisor-employee relationships. Relationships that endure rest on fair, mutually beneficial, agreed-upon expectations and responsibilities that apply to both supervisors and employees.

I can best introduce the basic partnering procedure by describing how I discovered its effectiveness. The procedure grew out of a system of extraordinarily effective family communication procedures that my wife, Jeanie, my daughter Shann, and I worked out when Shann was a teenager. We had started giving Shann an allowance when she was eight. Three years later, we negotiated an oral agreement that she would do specified household chores in return. I believed that writing and signing something would result in clearer and more precise expectations and commitments. But Jeanie and Shann thought that would imply mistrust.

With each year's review of the allowance and chores, I became more certain that Shann's only commitment was to collect her allowance each month. During our reviews, she readily agreed to the chores. When it came time to do them, especially to clean her room, mother and daughter usually did serious battle. Shann didn't care that her room was in disarray, but Jeanie wanted it to look as neat and clean as the rest of the house. Shann would say that she got her chores done and Jeanie would snap back, "Yes, but only after I'm at my wit's end and have threatened you in some way. I always have to say something to get you to do them that I hate myself for later."

When Shann was fourteen, she and Jeanie thought of a radical approach to resolve the problem. They suggested increasing Shann's allowance enough that she could manage her own money and pay all her own direct expenses. For the money and freedom of choice, Shann was to do specified scheduled chores. They even offered to put the details in writing.

To make sure that Shann was comfortable with the agreement, I asked her to write it, so she wouldn't feel stuck with our words. She agreed, but found it nearly impossible to write it on her own. Then I prepared an outline to which Shann added the details. It took her two weeks to complete her first draft. The three of us reviewed and discussed it several times until we were all comfortable with it. That outline and the discussions inspired my concept of drafting partnering agreements that individuals could adapt to their needs.

Jeanie and I were amazed at how much it helped us as a team to spell out what we expected of Shann. From then on, the two of us functioned as one in our leadership role with Shann. That alone made life much easier and more satisfying for all three of us.

Shann was hesitant when we discussed signing the agreement. Through that dialogue, she discovered that she feared being held accountable when circumstances beyond her control prevented her from accomplishing her chores on schedule. That discovery caused Jeanie and me to recognize the draft for what it was, a list of our demands.

Shann wanted to feel encouraged to negotiate schedule changes when needed. That was a proactive stance that caused us to look at the nature of our support for her. We realized that it would not be fair to ask her to accomplish anything for which we were not willing to provide the support she needed. We wanted her to be empowered by the document, not intimidated. So we added four items to the document. We agreed to respond to Shann's potential desire to reschedule her chores by listening to her reasoning before commenting on her requests. We agreed that we would honor her requests when her reasoning was sound. We agreed to provide all the support she needed to accomplish her chores. And we encouraged her to let us know any time she felt that either of us was being controlling in any aspect of our relationship with her.

These additions inspired me to make leadership support commitments integral to partnering agreements. The items also caused the three of us to agree to a stipulation that Shann would forfeit five dollars each time she procrastinated on her chores. With those modifications, all three of us felt comfortable about signing the agreement. I said to Shann, "If any of us is uncomfortable signing, it means that potential hassles exist. When we know about them before they occur, we can prevent them or reduce the negative consequences when they do happen."

During the following year, Jeanie asked Shann only twice when Shann was going to do an overdue chore. When the exchanges became argumentative, I asked Shann. "Does this mean that you are ready to forfeit five dollars?" Both times, Shann answered no and immediately did the chore without visible irritation or further words.

Those events led to another discovery. We no longer had to beg and badger Shann to accomplish her commitments. We accomplished what we all wanted by periodically asking what kind of help might be useful to her. That question later became a profound revelation to me about management practices. I discovered that a person who asked an employee, "What additional leadership support can you use?" was a leader of people, while a person who did not ask it was a controller of people.

Shann, Jeanie, and I reviewed and revised our agreement every year. The formal working relationship gave Shann a new sense of responsibility and accountability, and it increased our trust in her judgment. The results of that agreement have continued to guide and enrich our relationship with Shann and now with her family.

Jeanie and I discovered that putting our mutual commitments in writing and leading the negotiations to get the agreement signed were true leadership practices. They were not controlling supervisory practices because they put Shann on the one hand, and Jeanie and me as a team, on the other hand, in control of our respective parts of the agreement. Even asking Shann if she preferred to forfeit five dollars when she started to renege on her commitment was a leadership practice. It left Shann in control because she was free to choose her response. Our negotiations with her over schedule changes were also acts of leadership. Our agreement made it simple, easy, and extraordinarily satisfying for Jeanie and me to follow effective leadership practices such as good communication and behavior modeling in our relationship with Shann. Similarly, partnering procedures are based on principles that keep both supervisors and employees in control of their respective parts of the partnering agreement.

Moreover, the procedures are simple and effective. Any supervisor can follow them, and all supervisors who do will be effective leaders.

Few organizations will thrive in the future without optimum quality and productivity accomplished through synergistic work relationships. No organization, industry, institution, or government agency can have synergistic work relationships without empowered and committed employees. Employees do not empower themselves, nor can they be trained to be empowered. Organizations do not empower employees. Supervisors (or leaders), those who have immediate power over employees (or direct reports), are the ones who must empower employees. Partnering creates synergistic leader-direct-report relationships in which both parties share and increase their total power.

Employee partnering is relevant to all organizations and all jobs. It is needed wherever people depend on each other. The two-person company, the one thousand-employee company, and the one hundred thousand-employee company all need partnering, as do the family members of a privately owned company, the employees of a publicly owned company, or the employees of a nonprofit organization. Partnering is needed between leaders and direct reports whether they are in the same office or separated by continents. Partnering is a communication tool, and communication is a universal need. Partnering works at every level of management in any kind of organized group.

Audience

This book is written for human relations specialists, academics, and leaders in business, industry, and government. My vision is that work will nurture employees as well as compensate them. Supervisors will share their power and have more influence and success. Customer satisfaction and profits will increase in proportion to employee job satisfaction, not at the expense of it. The ultimate goal of this book is to improve the financial, mental, and physical health of employees and the profitability of employers. It is my hope that human relations professionals who understand employee partnering will connect with enlightened leaders in business, industry, government, and education. Teams resulting from those connections will institute employee partnering in the leaders' organizations. This book can bring these professionals and enlightened leaders together and guide them in implementing employee partnering.

Although anyone who is a supervisor or who trains supervisors can use this book, internal and external human resource, organizational development, and training professionals are the primary audience. They are the persons charged with developing and implementing quality and productivity improvement, pay-for-performance, and other performance improvement programs. Because partnering with employees is the foundation for performance improvement, encouraging partnering can be a mission for all human relations-oriented professions.

Recently, while auditing a Total Quality Management (TQM) workshop, I heard a company president ask the workshop leader three simple yet profound questions. He said, "I really learned a lot, and I like what I learned. But how do we get our employees to understand and commit to Total Quality Management? How do we get employees to understand what's in it for them? How do we get employees to believe TQM is not just another management fad?" Despite his perception that he had learned a great deal, he had no clue about how to work with his employees to implement TQM. The workshop leader responded by reviewing the workshop topics. He made no reference to the win-lose orientation displayed in the questioner's assumption that management had to "get employees to understand." At the end of the review, the president did not realize that his questions had not been addressed.

Questions that reveal a need for redirection and answers that do not offer any redirection are more the rule than the exception in efforts to implement quality improvement programs. Management needs professional guidance to answer tough questions like these. *Partnering with Employees* offers a simple, practical, low-cost, and highly effective system that professionals can readily use to lead the way when management cultures must be transformed.

The organizations that will be successful in the future need enlightened leaders and managers who want to transform their management cultures now. Enlightened leaders and managers are people who seriously want to improve working relationships, customer satisfaction, and profits within their spheres of influence. They feel a deep discontent with the status quo. They are always open to consideration of the pros and cons of new management philosophies and procedures. Leaders and managers who can decide to implement employee partnering and to team up with human relations professionals to accomplish it are also a primary audience for this book.

Overview of the Contents

The Introduction explains how people become programmed toward win-lose relationships. When work relationships are adversarial, win-lose programming is a primary underlying cause. Part One (Chapters One through Four) explains the concepts and principles of the partnering system. Chapter One describes my research about causes of relationship problems between supervisors and employees and provides interactive exercises that illustrate employee partnering concepts and lead readers through the basic partnering procedures. The chapter also lists the primary performance improvement benefits that partnering generates. Chapter Two explains three key human relations principles and how they support employee partnering. Examples drawn from real situations illustrate how the principles produce exceptionally satisfying and effective partnering. Chapter Three explains three key principles for conducting partnering negotiations and includes practical examples of negotiations. Chapter Four presents case studies illustrating implementation of partnering agreements. The chapter addresses the necessity of modeling partnering from the top down and overcoming employee mistrust of management, and it discusses how to deal with management's concern that partnering might involve too much paperwork.

Part Two (Chapters Five through Seven) covers step-by-step procedures that anyone can follow to implement employee partnering. Chapter Five details the rationale and procedures that leaders can follow when partnering with direct reports, including guidance in negotiating with direct reports and details about the kinds of general support leaders can commit to provide. Leadership support effects the greatest change in work relationships. This chapter also describes how leaders can negotiate about their expectations for employees' achievement of objective and measurable results, and it discusses why a cosigned agreement ensures that potential differences have been or will be resolved. Chapter Six describes mutually satisfying and efficient employee performance reviews that support continuous improvement in employee and team performance. Effective reviews eliminate the one-sided judgments that make ordinary reviews distasteful and often useless for performance improvement. In the partnering system, all reviews result in team performance improvement plans. Chapter Seven explains discretionary leadership partnering procedures, which only some leaders must perform. Even though these procedures are at times necessary in all organizations, not all leaders will be responsible for carrying them out. The Appendix contains examples of how partnering agreements and procedures can help leaders and direct reports to pinpoint, document, and address the causes of low achievement.

Littleton, Colorado Duke Nielsen
May 1993

ACKNOWLEDGMENTS

The work that culminated in this book began in 1979. To adequately acknowledge all who have contributed to it over the years would take many pages. However, there are several people without whose support the work would never have been started or completed. I feel special gratitude and give recognition to Jeanie, my childhood sweetheart and lifelong partner, for loving me and encouraging me, in spite of my singlemindedness when working, and for sustaining us in times of need; to our daughter, Shann, our son-in-law, Jeff, and their children, Lauren, Nielsen, and Jacob, whose love, affection, enthusiasm, and hope for the future make it worthwhile to go to any lengths to improve this world for future generations; and to my mother, my sister, Darlene, and brother, Harry, for their love and confidence in me. I also owe much to my father and my happy memory of him.

My uncle Johnny and Earl Hartwigsen showed me that work provides the greatest opportunity for daily self-fulfilling achievements and nurturing relationships. The leader-helper and love-of-work relationships that I had with them in my youth are the philosophical models that guided my development of employee partnering.

Art Prado and Rick Feinberg, friends extraordinaire and coauthors with me on other works, whose companionship, conversations, questioning, and above all, integrity have inspired my search for simplicity and practicality in this book, were also models for the kind of leadership I describe.

Kent Kopen, a young manager and intellectual kindred spirit who was the first to implement employee partnering agreements with his employees, produced results beyond our highest expectations. He continues to "jump start" me every time we converse. Gordon Starbuck, now deceased, was the contractor who chaired the committees that spent three years reviewing the formative stages of the partnering system. His friendship and assistance were inspiring. I also thank all the other women and men who have contributed to this book and who will share the credit for any success that it may have.

D. N.

THE AUTHOR

Duke Nielsen is president of Performance Systems, a management consulting firm in Littleton, Colorado. He received his B.S. degree (1957) in forestry from Iowa State University.

Nielsen started his research, writing, training, and consulting in the field of applied supervisory and leadership development. In 1979, his research shifted to performance-based compensation and then to employee partnering. He has been active in the American Society for Training and Development and the National Society for Performance and Instruction. In 1977, he received the American Society for Training and Development Torch Award for Original Training Program Development. Nielsen's previous books include *Job Supervisory Training* (1974); *Construction: Opportunities and Risks,* a simulation for operating companies (1975, with A. Prado); *Supervisory Training for Foremen* (1977); *Leadership and Communication for Supervisors* (1978); *Performance-Based Compensation* (1979, with R. Feinberg); *Performance Engineering* (1983); and *Managing Without Manipulating* (1990).

From 1972 to 1987, Nielsen was director of education and training for Associated General Contractors of Colorado. He developed and marketed concepts and provided staff support for the Associated General Contractors of America Education Committee when it initiated and developed the association's widely recognized Supervisory Training Program. He provided the same services for the association's Manpower and Training Committee when it initiated and developed the association's Construction Craft Skills Training programs, used by secondary and postsecondary schools and by industry nationwide.

Introduction

The Benefits of Win-Win Work Relationships

Employee partnering is based on negotiated agreements for support and achievement that replace job descriptions and eliminate win-lose transactions between supervisors and employees. These agreements are not contracts. Instead, they recognize a covenant of good faith. They formalize the expectations that partners have of each other and the commitments they make to each other, and they transform supervisor-employee relationships into leader-direct report relationships.

The philosophy and principles for partnering between organizations and for partnering between leaders and direct reports are the same because relationship problems between organizations and between supervisors and employees have a common origin: win-lose struggles for power and control. Just as partnering agreements between organizations establish a new basis for trust, respect, and cooperation and recognize the legitimate interests of both parties, partnering agreements between leaders and direct reports create similar, lasting win-win relationships. These relationships are the synergies that will create win-win results for all stakeholders in organizations of the future. Synergistic leader–direct-report relationships are essential if organizations are to respond to rapid changes in customer demands and to thrive in the new world economy.

Win-Lose Programming

Everyone seeks power to control circumstances and satisfy his or her needs and wants. Most people are programmed from the time they are born to participate in predominantly win-lose struggles for power and control. The programming starts when parents act to control their children's first responsive behavior. It is reinforced when more-powerful siblings beat out less-powerful siblings in contests for attention or any other desirable object. The reinforcement continues in virtually all relationships, even the most loving and ideal ones.

For example, my son-in-law, Jeff, has coached youth league football for eight seasons, with me as one of his assistants for the last two seasons. His teams have been in the league's super bowl three times. The players and their parents love him as a person and as a coach because he is kind, principled, and patient.

How important are these characteristics in programming others? By a wide margin, in a secret ballot his eight year old son, Nielsen, received from his teammates the highest number of votes for team captain. I am certain the reason is that Nielsen's relationship with teammates is a reflection of his dad's loving and principled relationship with the players.

Nevertheless, even though Jeff and I model good leadership behavior most of the time, we do too much win-lose programming. When the little players' lack of attention and other poor behavior in practice sessions stretches our patience past the breaking point, we yell at the players, mildly threatening them in order to control their performance.

When we do this, we are using power to control them. In response to our outbursts, the kids show hurt, confusion, indifference, resistance, or defiance, but regardless of their response, they see that "good guys" use power to control others, especially when the good guys are under stress. In the players' eyes, our modeling makes win-lose behavior "right."

Power-and-control, or win-lose, programming is reinforced by participation in win-lose contests. Contests of all kinds are mainstays of recreation and entertainment and are necessary for mental and physical health. Winning is a positive goal. Being part of a winning team is especially satisfying. Yet contests by definition are win-lose; in order for a person or a team to win, another person or team has to lose. The damage these win-lose contests cause is not the result of the failure that people experience in losing, because most learning comes from failed attempts to make progress. The damage is that win-lose contests inhibit participants from discovering the possibility and the value of win-win situations. This is not to suggest contests are bad. It is to point out that our human relations programming is overwhelmingly shaped by win-lose situations and that this lopsided programming is a powerful and mostly destructive influence in all of our relationships.

Win-Win Programming

Of course, there are also opportunities for us to learn about win-win situations. For example, the fourth and fifth graders in my granddaughter Lauren's grade school elected classmates to be school-ground mediators. The criterion for nominating these mediators was their observed inclination to mediate confrontations in their ordinary classroom and recess activities. The elected students took training after school for several weeks to understand mediation and to accomplish it on the playground. My granddaughter was one of those elected. When I arrived at the school gym for the mediators' graduation from training, I fell into conversation with a man whose grandson was also in the group and who was surprised when I said my granddaughter was a mediator. He remarked, "I don't see how girls can intimidate other kids enough to get the job done."

His attitude illustrated precisely the power-and-control programming that causes win-lose relationship problems. "Intimidation may have its place in some circumstances, but it has nothing to do with mediation. Intimidation is exactly the opposite of mediation," I told him, and when the graduate mediators came out on the stage to start the awards ceremony, the makeup of the group made my day. Of the thirty-three beaming fourth and fifth graders, only six were boys.

The twenty-seven girls elected by their classmates demonstrated the youngsters' comprehension of the complex job of mediation. The fourth and fifth graders showed a more advanced understanding of productive human relations than did the grandfather I spoke to. They understood the need for listening and communication skills in human relations. The numbers made it clear that more girls than boys demonstrated those qualities, which appears to support the popular premise that in general females tend to use more discussion and mediation than men do to get their needs met. The vote result was a proof that win-lose human relations programming can be overcome.

The Distinction Between Power and Control

Win-lose programming is especially destructive in modern-day work relationships. In combination with supervisory training, this programming causes supervisors to be only kinder and gentler manipulators. Adversarial work relationships stem from a colossal misunderstanding: power and control are perceived to be the same when, in fact, they are distinctly different.

Having power is fundamental to survival and to legitimate success (success not at someone else's expense). Having power *and* controlling resources is necessary for many worthwhile purposes, including control of costs, equipment, and natual resources. Even controlling people in times of immediate danger, such as military battles, riots, and earthquakes, is appropriate. But using power to control human resources in organizations in these times of advanced human rights, is increasingly damaging and wasteful. In work relationships, win-lose struggles over control prevent employee empowerment and make quality improvement programs difficult to implement and sustain. These struggles nearly always produce lose-lose results in the long term for supervisors, employees, and their organizations. Even so, because having power is critical to survival and success, power is an essential ingredient in partnering with employees.

Empowering employees does not mean that supervisors give power away. It means that they share power with employees. Supervisors and employees make joint use of power, and no one loses power. Empowered employees are not turned loose to do their own thing or to be out of control. By empowering employees, supervisors change from controlling to being in control.

Controlling means manipulating employees' performance. *Being in control* means negotiating whenever appropriate, but always being in control of what one agrees to do. In partnering, supervisors are always in control of what they agree to allow employees to do. They are always in control of what they agree to provide in the way of employee support. What makes partnering a win-win solution is that empowered employees are also in control of what they agree to do. Win-win cultures produce a win for all organizational stakeholders.

The change from controlling to being in control is a paradigm shift that converts supervisors into true leaders. Employee partnering changes a supervisor's mission from getting his or her subordinates to do what the supervisor wants them to do to providing the practical support that makes direct reports' jobs more satisfying and productive.

Most enlightened managers know that modern organizations need win-win cultures. Authors, consultants, and trainers have expressed that need for several decades in management books, articles, and workshops. The human relations model of win-win relationships is advocated by W. Edwards Deming, a founding father of Total Quality Management (Deming, 1986); management theorist Peter F. Drucker (1989), who describes the model as the basis for "information based organizations" of the future; and performance quality gurus, Philip B. Crosby (1984) and Joseph M. Juran (1964), who see this model as the basis on which quality is built.

Tom Peters and R. H. Waterman, Jr. (1982), James M. Kouzes and Barry Z. Posner (1987), and Peters (1987) describe the human relations model. Stephen R. Covey's *The Seven Habits Of Highly Effective People* (1989) presents a personal application of the model and Peter M. Senge (1990) offers a systematic perspective on it that he calls "the learning organization." Peter Block (1987) exposes the political manipulation that marks win-lose organizational cultures and contrasts that manipulation with the virtues of the empowering human relations model. Block's book is a virtual prescription for the procedures in this book. It is now time to move partnering from the realm of theory and prescription to widespread organizational practice.

Win-Lose Language

Language is a major part of culture. Words used in conversation and in literature reflect attitudes and biases that foster work cultures. The words *manager, supervisor,* and *subordinate* reflect the way power is perceived and used in win-lose work relationships. These words promote the use of power to manipulate and control people. A manager controls and manipulates resources. A supervisor oversees workers, and supervision is mostly an act of enforcement. Subordinate is a subservient title because subordinates are under the authority of superiors or supervisors. A new vocabulary is necessary to define a new model of relationships, to awaken people to the new model, and to foster implementation of the model as the basis for win-win work relationships.

Win-Win Language

In support of win-win management cultures, I prefer to use the terms *leader, direct report,* and *employee* to depict employee partnering relationships. Leaders inspire, guide, and support people who report to them. Direct reports answer to leaders and receive direction and support from leaders, but direct reports are partners with their leaders, not servants to them.

Part One

PARTNERING BASICS

1

Putting Mutual Expectations, Commitments, and Good Faith in Writing

This chapter will explain the fundamental supervisor-subordinate relations problem in organizations, describe the partnering procedures in an actual partnering experience, and explain how partnering makes ordinary performance improvement efforts seventy times more productive.

Supervisor-Subordinate Relations Research

I stated in the Preface that my research showed that managers and supervisors made little practical use of what they learned in human relations training. What follows describes that research, pinpoints the specific causes of supervisor-subordinate relationship problems, and shows that the causes stem from win-lose management practices, not from individual supervisors. All my references to supervisory shortcomings relate to a systemic management dilemma. I am not pointing a finger at individuals.

The initial subjects of my research were the more than eighty thousand participants who completed human relations training that I developed. (I personally taught more than three thousand of these people, who worked in the construction industry, health services, other service industries, manufacturing, education, and state and local governments. More than sixty-four thousand participants completed written evaluations at the end of the last sessions of their training classes. They rated their learning experience an average of 8.8 on a scale of 0 to 10. Thirty-two thousand of these evaluations were usable as data samples and were compiled and analyzed.

More than half of the eighty thousand participants also took related serial training. Other instructors and I asked these repeat participants, "To what extent are you implementing the human relations practices you learned in the previous related classes?" Instructors took notes on the ensuing discussions, which I later compared with my own notes. Nearly all participants' responses described disappointment. The consensus in every group discussion on this question was that the participants were applying less than 10 percent of what they learned. Even worse, the application diminished as time passed. While participants liked what they learned, the training rarely reduced and usually increased their supervisory frustrations. The participants said they now understood more about good work relations but rarely had enough time or support on the job to apply what they had learned. Because they felt guilty for not practicing what they learned, the long-term effect of their learning was greater frustration with their work relationships.

Early in this research, I analyzed instructors' notes and participants' written feedback, from which I hypothesized the root causes of subordinates' not meeting supervisors' expectations. The initial cause statements were tested with subsequent class groups and revised many times until the following basic causes became clear. The frequency noted for each cause represents consensus demonstrated in class discussions of the reasons why participants did not implement what they learned.

1. Subordinates are unclear about supervisors' achievement expectations and have insufficient supervisory support to accomplish those expectations. Frequency: 89 percent.
2. Subordinates have inadequate knowledge or skill to achieve as expected. Frequency: 9.5 percent.
3. Subordinates are incapable of learning to achieve or physically incapable of achieving as expected. Frequency: 0.5 percent
4. Subordinates understand supervisors' expectations but are not committed to accomplishing them. Frequency: 1 percent.

Whenever any employee's accomplishment is below expectations, it is the result of one or more of these four causes. The relative frequency of the causes pinpoints the mistaken beliefs that perpetuate win-lose management cultures. Nearly all the individuals in the training-class discussions said they assumed that employees were at fault for all achievement shortcomings. They also assumed that employees were responsible for taking the initiative to improve performance. However, the first three causes show that these two assumptions are wrong 99 percent of the time.

As cause one reveals, supervisors are the source of both achievement expectations and support. Therefore, only supervisors can be responsible for ensuring that their expectations are communicated and understood. Only supervisors can provide the support employees need to achieve supervisors' expectations. And only supervisors can reduce the 89 percent frequency of this cause. It is supervisors' responsibility to initiate action that will remedy performance problems caused by lack of understanding or support.

Sometimes needed support is not available or is impractical. In those cases, supervisors have to adjust their expectations to that which they can and will support. Such adjustments make it possible for employees to meet expectations.

Employees can take the initiative to request clearer supervisory expectations and more support, and in perfect leader-direct-report relationships, they would do so. However, there are few perfect work relationships, so employees rarely make such requests. Even employees who have the courage to ask often do not know what to ask for because they do not know what they do not know. Therefore, taking the initiative to clarify and communicate expectations and determine the need for support must be leaders' responsibility.

In perfect work relationships, direct reports also know when they lack knowledge or skill (frequency, 9.5 percent). In reality, when direct reports' achievement is low, they are often not aware of its level or do not know why it is low. Furthermore, in win-lose cultures, employees commonly fear that requests for knowledge or skills training might draw supervisors' attention (and wrath) to employee shortcomings. Thus, the responsibility to initiate action to determine lack of knowledge or skill and to guide employees' learning also belongs to supervisors. In short, any supervisory response to causes one and two must emphasize an initiative to start remedial action, not personal faultfinding.

The same rationale applies to capability. It is desirable to have employees admit when they are incapable of achieving expectations. However, in win-lose cultures, expecting such admissions is wishful thinking. The responsibility for initiating action to determine an employee's lack of physical or mental capability also belongs to supervisors. Here, too, the emphasis must be on an initiative to start remedial action, not on whose fault the problem is.

When supervisors base their efforts to improve employee performance on the common erroneous assumptions that employees are solely responsible for improvement, they manipulate employees. To continuously improve their own performances, employees have to want to improve. To want to improve, employees have to feel ownership for their performance deficiencies. But lack of understanding and support, of knowledge or skill, or of capability causes 99 percent of persistent low achievement. These problems must be addressed first by people's leaders. Employees cannot own what is not theirs to own.

When supervisors make it clear that they believe employees cause their own failures, they leave employees feeling helpless and guilty for failing to please their supervisors. Moreover, there is no way for these employees to win or to resolve the guilt. As a result, many employees resist supervision, suffer stress, experience discrimination or harassment, file grievances, produce work of low quality and quantity, and feel no loyalty. It is important to note that most supervisors are also direct reports to their own supervisors. It is necessary, therefore, to understand these comments from the perspectives of both leaders and direct reports.

Performance Evaluation as Employee Manipulation

Supervisors and employees typically dislike conducting performance reviews and rarely feel satisfied with review results. W. Edwards Deming, a living legend in the field of implementing Total Quality Management, describes "evaluation of performance, merit rating, or annual review" as one of the "Seven Deadly Diseases" of management (Deming, 1986).

The assumption that employees are at fault for low achievement is one factor that makes performance reviews manipulative, distressing, and counterproductive. The other factor is the lack of a negotiated support and achievement agreement on which evaluations can be based. Employee partnering eliminates both problems. It creates ideal conditions for win-win leader–direct-report team reviews. Such reviews support continuous mutual improvement in both achievement and job satisfaction.

My research showed that lack of knowledge or skill causes 9.5 percent of employee low achievement. Since supervisors are also employees and direct reports themselves, and since the research covered many supervisory levels, cause two applies to supervisors in the same proportion as it does to their employees: that is, only 10 percent of supervisors' low achievement is due to lack of knowledge or skill. Yet the research surveys found that education and training programs make up nearly 100 percent of structured efforts to improve supervisory performance. This means that nearly 100 percent of structured supervisory performance improvement efforts apply to only 9.5 percent of the causes of supervisory performance deficiencies. Since win-lose struggles for power and control cause trainees to implement less than 10 percent of what they learn in ordinary human relations training programs, this training is only about one percent effective (10 percent of 9.5 percent). Moreover, even the 1 percent implementation of learned practices can be counterproductive. In win-lose cultures, the 1 percent improvement results in the phenomenon I mentioned earlier of supervisors' being kinder and gentler while controlling employees' performance.

Training alone has little potential to influence management cultures directly or to significantly diminish destructive win-lose practices. Wherever win-lose relationships dominate, they prevent nontechnical performance improvement efforts from producing long-term cost-effective benefits. However, my research does not question the value of human relations training. Instead, my message is that human relations training can be effective only in win-win organizational cultures.

Work Relationships: The Key to Performance

Work relationships are the products of expectations that supervisors and employees have of each other. They start with each party hoping for and expecting something from the other. People do not usually explain their expectations of each other to each other; they may not even be conscious of their own expectations. But expectations always exist and always influence relationships.

Research on the causes of low achievement shows that supervisors and employees base most of their performance expectations of each other on assumptions. Incorrect assumptions lead to incorrect expectations and influence supervisors to use their power to try to control employee performance. Controlling supervision is the root of job stress, waste, discrimination, grievances, harassment, employee sabotage, and so forth. Erroneous expectations perpetuate the four causes of low achievement and prevent implementation of most of the practices that people learn in human relations training.

The lesson is that where there are no written and agreed upon expectations for support and achievement between supervisors and employees, supportive work relationships have minimal chance to take root and grow. In the absence of supportive work relationships, any kind of performance improvement efforts that are influenced by supervisor-employee interactions, will probably not meet desired goals. This lesson is especially relevant to TQM. My studies show that the lack of defined and negotiated expectations is a fundamental but often missing part of TQM programs and makes implementing TQM unnecessarily slow, stressful, costly, and difficult to sustain.

The lack of defined and negotiated expectations is a root human relations problem that has to be solved in most organizations before there is much chance of accomplishing desired individual and organizational achievement. A major obstacle to solving this problem is that supervisors and employees usually do not know how to define and document their expectations or don't have time to do it even when they know how. This book describes procedures that eliminate this obstacle and solve the problem.

The most cost effective model for implementing partnering with employees has been to have trained internal or external consultants facilitate the implementation process. The consultants start implementation by identifying supervisors' achievement expectations for employees, identifying employees' expectations for support, and developing drafts that include both kinds of expectations. Drafts are given to employees and their supervisors to independently edit to their liking. After supervisors and employees edit their drafts, consultants facilitate meetings in which supervisors and their employees collaborate to negotiate and combine their edited expectations into one mutual agreement. This converts supervisors from enforcers into leaders and converts subordinates into truly empowered, creative, and self-motivated direct reports who are nurtured by supportive work relationships.

The following five interactive exercises will help readers to experience the procedures and the satisfaction of defining and negotiating support and achievement expectations. You can assume both roles and do the exercises by yourself or you can have another person (ideally, your direct report) assume one of the roles. Some information from the Preface and the Introduction is repeated in the first exercise for the benefit of your partner, who may not have read those sections.

Exercise One: Understanding the Need for Partnering with Employees

Instructions: (1) You and your partner individually read the following paragraphs and highlight or underline words and phrases that stand out for you. (2) Compare your responses to the issues.

Related Information. Partnering with employees calls for a major paradigm shift. Most people are programmed to seek power as a means for controlling others in order to satisfy their own needs and wants. The programming starts when parents coerce children to obey them. More-powerful siblings reinforce this programming when they compete for attention and win at the expense of less-powerful siblings. Competitive games and most sports further support this pattern of interaction, as do relations with most teachers and other adults. The win-lose orientation has been the predominant way of life throughout history.

Although win-lose attitudes produce good sports, people are beginning to realize that they also produce dysfunctional families, ineffective politics, and unproductive, costly work relationships. Managers are waking up to the fact that they may have authority but their control of others is a myth. The people who have real control are those who actually produce goods and deliver services. They are in the position to say yes or no. They can decide to work creatively and enthusiastically or reluctantly and without commitment. Managers need employees' cooperation and commitment to produce results. That commitment cannot be forced. It can only be inspired and empowered.

Partnering with employees requires win-win thinking. Partnering transforms controlled adversarial work relations into commitment-based work teams. It engages the critical thinking of leaders and direct reports and delivers responsibility to those who do the work. In leader–direct-report partnerships, dreaded performance reviews become eagerly anticipated opportunities to improve communication and achievement.

Partnering does not turn employees loose to do their own thing. It does not take control away from supervisors. Through partnering, supervisors change from enforcers to leaders, from controlling to being in control. *Controlling* means manipulating employees' performance. *Being in control* means negotiating whenever appropriate. Leaders are always in control of what they agree to allow employees to do, and they are always in control of deciding what support they agree to provide. What makes partnering a win-win situation is that employees are also in control of what they agree to do. Controlling is win-lose. Being in control is win-win. In partnering, leaders maintain control without controlling.

Win-lose mind-sets make performance evaluations manipulative and distasteful, human relations supervisory training 1 percent effective, and Total Quality Management (TQM) difficult to implement and sustain. Partnering mind-sets support continuous performance improvement, make ordinary improvement efforts up to seventy times more productive, and increase customer satisfaction and profits in proportion to employee job satisfaction, not at the expense of job satisfaction.

Issues to Consider.

- What problems do you see as being caused by supervisors controlling employees?
- What would it mean to your organization if all of its supervisors used their power to inspire, guide, and support their employees rather than control them?

Exercise Two: Negotiating Leadership Support

Instructions: (1) You and your partner individually read the following paragraphs. (2) Together, complete the numbered steps. (3) Compare your responses to the issues.

Related Information. The core activity in employee partnering is the negotiation of a win-win agreement for leader support and direct-report achievement. Such agreements require that both leaders and direct reports feel sufficiently empowered to express and promote their points of view on support and expectations. The empowering process is a *missing* component in most quality improvement efforts. Although empowerment is a primary focus of TQM, real empowerment is rarely accomplished even in fairly effective TQM efforts. Organizations cannot empower employees, nor can they train them to be empowered. People with immediate power over employees have to empower them. Empowerment is accomplished when people share power, not when one person gives power up to another. Leaders empower employees primarily by committing to leadership support.

The leadership support commitments requisite to productive and satisfying work relationships are listed in Exhibit 1.1. The negotiation of partnering agreements *always* starts with a discussion of this list. Leader–direct-report agreement on these support commitments empowers employees to be true partners when they negotiate commitments to achievement expectations. When a supervisor and a subordinate reach agreement on this list, they have taken the first step toward functioning as a true leader-direct-report team.

Using the Leadership Support Agreement. The leader goes through five steps to reach agreement with his or her direct report about the support the leader will provide.

Exhibit 1.1. Leadership Support Agreement

It is my leadership responsibility to make sure that you receive the support and resources that you need to accomplish your achievement commitments. Following are specific ways that I expect to keep abreast of your needs and to provide needed support:

1. I expect you to come to me with your problems. However, I expect you to have suggested solutions to discuss, not to leave the solutions to me. I will gladly discuss your proposed solutions and help you implement the ones we agree on.
2. I will regularly ask you for ideas to improve our team achievement. I will support the implementation of any ideas that you and I agree have potential value.
3. Should you ever find it difficult to accomplish your work because you and another person have a poor work relationship, and you want assistance to improve the relationship, I will facilitate discussions to assist you in accomplishing your goal.
4. I will promote interstaff (interdepartment) cooperation.
5. I will do whatever is necessary and reasonable to make needed equipment, material, and supplies available for you to accomplish your commitments.
6. I will resolve differences between us by negotiating win-win agreements with you.
7. I expect, and will welcome, constructive feedback on my support for your performance.
8. I will have regular discussions with you (frequency) ____________ in person or by phone, to keep up on the ways I can help you achieve your commitments.
9. Should you ever feel uncomfortable about discussing differences with me, I commit to invite a third party of your choice—from this company and acceptable to both of us—to facilitate the discussion. I also commit to seek a win-win resolution and to hold no grudges for your requesting a facilitated discussion.
10. When unforseen circumstances or new priorities cause me to change my expectations of you, I will negotiate adjustments with you.

The following signature (Leader) ____________ Date ________, acknowledges that the above leadership support commitments have been negotiated and mutually agreed to as a basis for this team's work relationship.

1. Read out loud the introductory paragraph and the first commitment. Ask your direct report, "Is this commitment important to you?" Acknowledge your report's answer. Then say, "I agree" or "I disagree." If you and your report disagree, discuss the item and negotiate an agreement to mark it Y to keep or D to delete it. Do this for all ten commitments.
2. Discuss whether support commitments that either you or your report think are important are missing from this list. Write in the missing commitments.
3. Look at commitment seven. Consider whether you need to change the wording to make it describe the way you both want to accomplish constructive feedback and write in changes if necessary. (In actual practice, you will consider changing the wording for each support commitment that you keep.)
4. When you and your report have negotiated the wording on all of the retained and added commitments, you as the leader sign the agreement.
5. Discuss how your commitment to these negotiated support items empowers your direct report to negotiate achievement expectations.

Issues to consider.

- What forms of resistance to support commitments do supervisors commonly show?
- What would you say to eliminate the resistance you just described?

Exercise Three: Negotiating Achievement Expectations

Instructions: (1) You and your partner individually, read the following paragraphs. (2) Together, complete the numbered steps. (3) Compare your responses to the issues.

Related Information. The negotiation of the leadership support items in the previous exercise empowers employees to be creative, assertive, and productive followers. But before employees can use that power to accomplish achievement expectations, leaders have to establish and document general areas of responsibility and define the excellent levels of achievement that they expect employees to attain. These expectations are not production objectives. Production objectives are quotas and are perceived by many organizations as necessary for efficient planning and scheduling but they rarely include any reference to support. When they are not met, they provide no means to focus on what aspect of performance to improve to increase production. Production objectives, therefore, are not necessary for effective partnering agreements. Therefore, the second step in functioning as a true leader is to negotiate direct report commitment to achievement expectations that support the leader-direct-report team's part of the organization's mission—including meeting production goals.

Exhibit 1.2 is a sample achievement expectation for a direct report which focuses on communication. Exhibit 1.3 illustrates an agreement that is used when a leader negotiates with his or her leader about what is expected of the junior leader in his or her leadership role. Completed partnering agreements will have ten to twenty-five expectations. Each expectation describes the general purpose of the achievement and lists the statements that describe excellent levels of achievement. A leader–direct-report team decides what level of achievement is appropriate for each statement. The data focus dialogue and produce mutual understanding of what excellent achievement is for each expectation. The completed statements define and confirm commitment and give direct reports a means to continually evaluate their own achievements. With these statements as a guide, people do not have to wait for a formal review to learn how they are doing. However, with partnering agreements in place, most people look forward to formal performance reviews because the data provide objective, fair, and useful criteria for win-win performance evaluations. (Exhibit 1.4 shows a completed achievement expectation.)

Exhibit 1.2. Direct Report Achievement Expectation: Communication

---

Top-performing companies have found ways to make sure that their people understand each other's instructions, expectations, goals, and priorities and all general communication.

It is my responsibility to be an effective link in the communication process within our company. This means taking the time and doing whatever is necessary to make sure that my leader, my direct reports, and other company personnel understand my communication and perform as expected.

It also means doing whatever is necessary for me to understand what others expect of me. I accomplish this communication by talking, listening, asking questions, and asking for tell-back to verify understanding.

I will have demonstrated excellent achievement of this expectation when:

a. Other people's performances show that my communication accomplishes its intended purpose ______ % of the time.
b. I provide information that other people need from me on a timely basis and recipients understand me as intended ______ % of the time.
c. I ask for tell-back to verify understanding ______ % of the time when there is a chance for misunderstanding.
d. I am sincere, candid, and honest ______ % of the time when I initiate information (or pass it on) and when I make requests.

Negotiated support: What specific support do I need from my leader in order to achieve this expectation? ______________________________

____
____
____
____

Exhibit 1.3. Direct-Report Achievement Expectation: Leadership

---

This company's policy is that all employees understand what areas of responsibility their leaders expect of them and what an excellent level of achievement is for each area of responsibility. Furthermore, employees are to be assured the support necessary for them to accomplish their achievement expectations. This enables them to be responsible for their work and for continuously improving their capability. As a leader, I am responsible for customizing predeveloped leadership support and achievement expectations to define the areas of responsibility and levels of achievement that I expect of my direct reports.

I will have demonstrated excellent achievement of this expectation when:

a. I have customized appropriate predeveloped leadership support commitments for ______ of my direct reports.
b. Excellent achievement levels for my direct reports are ambitious but realistic for ______ % of the expectations included in my partnering agreements with direct reports.
c. ______ % of my agreement drafts are ready as scheduled.

Negotiated support: What specific support do I need from my leader in order to achieve this expectation? ______________________________

____
____
____
____

Exhibit 1.4. Sample Completed Achievement Expectation: Communication

Top-performing companies have found ways to make sure that their people understand each other's instructions, expectations, goals, and priorities and all general communication.

It is my responsibility to be an effective link in the communication process within our company. This means taking the time and doing whatever is necessary to make sure that my leader, direct reports, and other company personnel understand my communication and perform as expected.

It also means doing whatever is necessary for me to understand what others expect of me. I accomplish it through talking, listening, asking questions, and asking for tell-back to verify understanding.

I will have demonstrated excellent achievement of this expectation when:

a. Other people's performances show that my communication accomplishes its intended purpose 90 % of the time.
b. I provide information that other people need from me on a timely basis and recipients understand me as intended 90 % of the time.
c. I ask for tell-back to verify understanding 95 % of the times when there is a chance for misunderstanding.
d. I am sincere, candid, and honest 95 % of the time when I initiate information (or pass it on) and when I make requests.

Negotiated support: What specific support do I need from my leader in order to achieve this expectation? ______________________________

____

____

____

____

Using the Direct-Report Achievement Expectation Agreement. The direct report follows these four steps to set each achievement expectation, using agreement drafts made up by consultants and provided to leaders and direct reports.

1. Read (out loud) the general purpose of the expectation. Then say, "I am comfortable with this," or "I would be comfortable with this if . . ." Describe the change you would like. Leader says, "I agree," or "I'm not comfortable with your conclusions." If the leader disagrees, negotiate a resolution and write in the changes.
2. Read (out loud) excellent achievement statement (a). Offer the percentage or other appropriate data that you think defines what excellent *but realistic* achievement might be. Do not try to define the level you think you are achieving now. If the leader is not comfortable with your suggestion, negotiate a mutually acceptable level and record it. Do the same for statements (b), (c), and (d).
3. Together, brainstorm the specific kind of support the direct report needs in order to accomplish this expectation at the level negotiated. Record the negotiated support.
4. Discuss the content of the signature page shown in Exhibit 1.5. Both of you sign it and discuss what it means to you to sign the agreement.

Exhibit 1.5. Agreement Signature Page.

This is to acknowledge that the individuals whose signatures follow have negotiated the leadership support commitments and direct report expectations in this partnering agreement to the best of their ability. They have agreed that all these commitments together represent a win-win working agreement for each of them. Their signatures are evidence of their mutual commitment to this agreement.

The parties to this agreement do not intend this document to imply a legal contract but a recognition that every employment includes an implied covenant of mutual good faith. This employee partnering agreement defines the criteria for good faith between leaders and employees. It is intended to establish work relationships in which trust and teamwork prevent disputes, foster cooperative bonds, and accomplish customer satisfaction, job satisfaction, and employer profitability.

(Employer) ______________________ does not intend this document to imply an employment agreement. (Employer) ______________________ does not intend to imply and does not guarantee that it will discharge employees only for failure to substantially meet the achievement expectations negotiated herein, or for other or just good cause. Notwithstanding any other provision of this agreement, all employment in this organization shall be employment at will.

(Leader) ________________________________ (Date) __________
(Employee) ______________________________ (Date) __________

Issues to Consider.

- Why is it important to agree on the numbers to put in the blanks?
- What happens if employees say they need support that leaders cannot provide?

Exercise Four: Achievement Reviews and Performance Improvement Plans

Instructions: (1) You and your partner individually read the following paragraphs. (2) Together, complete the numbered steps.

Related Information. The employee partnering philosophy for performance reviews is that every review for every employee will result in a performance improvement plan. The only question people should have going into a review is which performance expectations will have the greatest payoff for the organization, the direct report, and the leader when the expectation is achieved.

No matter how high or low employees' overall performance is rated, all employees should always be working on an active performance improvement plan with the support of their leaders. Even individuals who have maximum ratings on every expectation should have active performance improvement plans. This eliminates the perception that only bad performance calls for focused improvement efforts. Partnering improves good performances just as much as poor performances. It meets organizations' need for all employees to continuously improve.

Negotiated mutual expectations are the basis for team achievement reviews in which leaders' support performances and reports' achievement performances are both evaluated. Although each review initially focuses on employee achievement, supervisory shortcomings are automatically addressed and remedied along with employee shortcomings in the development of team performance improvement plans.

On the back of each Achievement Expectation Agreement is a Review of Support and Achievement form (Exhibit 1.6), which contains a rating guide.

Exhibit 1.6. Review of Support and Achievement.

Recalling team performance: In the appropriate sections below, list the pertinent information that will help you discuss performance of this expectation.

Leader's notes for achievement: ______________________________

____

____

____

Leader's notes for support: ______________________________

____

____

____

Direct report's notes for achievement: ______________________________

____

____

____

Direct report's notes for support: ______________________________

____

____

____

Customized Rating Guide

	Level 1 (Very low)	*Level 2 (Less than excellent)*	*Level 3 (Excellent)*	*Level 4 (Exceptional)*
a.	______	______	______	______
b.	______	______	______	______
c.	______	______	______	______
d.	______	______	______	______

Rate achievement levels. On the basis of your notes and the percentages listed in the customized rating guide, rate the direct report's actual achievement levels (one, two, three, or four) for the achievement statements (a), (b), (c), and (d) that appear on the front of this sheet. Record the levels here: (a) ______, (b) ______, (c) ______, (d) ______. Compute and record the average achievement rating: ______.

Determine causes of inadequate achievement for expectations rated below three. Discuss and agree on which of the following four causes contributed most to the low-achievement level for this expectation: (1) insufficient understanding or support ______, (2) insufficient knowledge or skill ______, (3) insufficient capability ______, (4) insufficient commitment ______. In the comments section below, record the ideas that you discussed.

Comments ______________________________

____

____

____

The percentages or other data in the excellent achievement statements are the basis for customizing this rating guide. Use the sample completed in Exhibit 1.7 and the number ranges in Table 1.1 to customize a guide for your negotiated numbers for each expectation. The guide is keyed to expectation statements (a), (b), (c), and (d). Once the percentage that indicates excellent achievement (level three) has been agreed upon, the percentages for very low achievement (level one), less-than-excellent achievement (level two), and exceptional achievement (level four) can be filled in from Table 1.1.

Conducting a Review of Support and Achievement. To practice using this review, leaders and direct reports can imagine that their agreement has been in operation for three months and complete the following six steps.

Exhibit 1.7. Completed Rating Guide.

Level 1 (Very low)	*Level 2 (Less than excellent)*	*Level 3 (Excellent)*	*Level 4 (Exceptional)*
a. 73–79	80–86	87–90–93	94–100
b. 73–79	80–86	87–90–93	94–100
c. 88–90	91–93	94–95–96	97–100
d. 88–90	91–93	94–95–96	97–100

Table 1.1. Rating Guide Customizing Aid.

Negotiated Level	*Level 1 (Low)*	*Level 2 (Not Bad)*	*Level 3 (Excellent)*	*Level 4 (Exceptional)*
100	100	100	100	100
99	97	98	99	100
98	94-95	96-97	98-99	100
97	91-93	94-96	97-98	99-100
96	89-91	92-94	95-97	98-100
95	88-90	91-93	94-96	97-100
94	82-86	87-91	92-96	97-100
93	81-85	86-90	91-95	96-100
92	78-83	84-89	90-95	96-100
91	74-80	81-87	88-94	95-100
90	73-79	80-86	87-93	94-100
89	69-76	77-84	85-92	93-100
88	66-74	75-83	84-92	93-100
87	65-73	74-82	83-91	92-100
86	64-72	73-81	82-90	91-100
85	63-71	72-80	81-89	90-100
80	55-64	65-74	75-85	86-100
75	38-52	53-67	68-82	83-95
70	33-45	44-59	60-77	78-90
60	30-39	40-49	50-70	71-85
50	20-29	30-42	43-58	61-75

1a. (To be completed by the leader.) Record, in the spaces provided, your perception of your report's achievement of the communication expectation and your perception of how you supported your report's communication performance.
1b. (To be completed by the direct report.) Record, in the spaces provided, your perception of your communication achievement and your perception of your leader's support of your communication performance.
2. Independently use the customized rating guide that you created for the expectation to select the range of percentages (or other appropriate data ranges) that best describes your perceptions of the achievement of this expectation over the last three months. In practice, that customized rating guide would be part of the review form that you are now using.
3. Independently record the level numbers of the selected percentages in the blanks below the rating guide. Average them for an overall achievement rating and record the number: ____ .
4. Exchange your achievement ratings with each other. In practice, both sets of numbers would be recorded on a table that lists all the achievement expectations that were agreed upon. (See Table 1.2.) Leaders and their reports would have this dual list of numbers to study for several days before the review meeting.
5. Look at the sample ratings in Table 1.2. Which two would you select to work on for improvement? Why? In practice, you would follow the instructions in the Support and Achievement Review to discuss and determine the most likely causes of the low achievement ratings.
6. In actual practice, you would also discuss potential remedies for the causes you chose.

Five: Implementation Procedures

Implementing partnering with all employees is much less difficult and much less time consuming than implementing traditional performance improvement programs. Instructions: 1) You and your partner individually read the following steps. 2) Discuss your perceptions and questions.

1. An internal or external facilitator acquires organization job titles and an understanding of how the company operates. With this information, the facilitator creates partnering agreement drafts for each participating direct report and the leader of each participating report. The drafts are put into three ring loose-leaf binders. This process should take approximately one week per sixteen employees.
2. Agreement drafts are distributed to participants. Each employee has his or her own copy. Leaders also have copies all in one binder for each of their reports. All recipients are given one week to study their copies, mark them

Table 1.2. Table of Achievement Ratings

	Expectations for Administrative Assistant	*Performance Review Ratings* *Leader's Rating*	*Direct Report's Rating*
1	Communication	3.0	3.0
2	Policies and procedures	3.4	3.0
3	Planning and organizing	1.3	2.0
4	Word processing	2.9	2.8
5	Purchasing office supplies	3.3	3.0
6	Administering petty cash fund	3.4	3.0
7	Supporting meetings	2.6	2.6
8	Taking dictation	3.3	3.0
9	Preparing correspondence	3.0	2.6
10	Preparing reports	3.0	2.6
11	Processing mail	3.3	2.6
12	Drafting support and achievement expectations	2.9	3.0
13	Negotiating support and achievement expectations	2.0	2.0
14	Cosigning support and achievement expectations	4.0	4.0
15	Conducting team achievement reviews	3.0	2.5
16	Determining causes of shortcomings	3.0	3.0
17	Preparing improvement plans	2.5	3.0
18	Negotiating acceptance adverse actions	N A	N A
19	Supporting achievement-based compensation	N A	N A
20	Interviewing and evaluating job applicants	3.5	3.0
21			
22			
23			
24			
25			

for suggested changes, and record initial data in the blanks for defining excellent achievement.

3. In eight-hour sessions, groups of leaders and their direct reports (up to sixteen people) meet with the facilitator, begin negotiating the final language of their support and achievement expectations and sign their partnering agreements. If people are unable to complete all of their expectations in the session, they finish them at their convenience, either one on one or one leader meeting with several reports.
4. The facilitator incorporates the negotiated changes and the excellent achievement percentages into final drafts and distributes these drafts. Computer disks containing all final drafts may also be prepared. This way the facilitator does all the paperwork for a turnkey operation. A trained facilitator will maintain quality control, meet schedule commitments, and assure that everyone gets the right material. Once the process is im-

plemented, no facilitators are needed to sustain it. Leaders and direct reports can easily update the agreements on their own after each periodic achievement review.

5. About thirty days after the facilitator delivers the final drafts, the same groups meet again with the facilitator in eight-hour group sessions for a team achievement review. Partners discuss perceptions of how their actual achievement compares to their negotiated expectations and support commitments. After discussing all of the expectations, they select one or two for which they develop improvement plans.
6. Four to six months after the first achievement review, leaders conduct their second team achievement reviews and prepare further performance improvement plans. In the process of comparing perceptions of achievement, the teams will renegotiate support and achievement exceptations as necessary.
7. Immediately following the second review, the facilitator leads a follow-up session of up to fifty participants to discuss questions, problems, successes, and general learning.

Identifying Achievement Expectations

Many achievement expectations are unique to each job title. My firm has built an extensive data base of these expectations. This section identifies leadership expectations and provides some guidance, in the form of a comparison with job description items, for defining direct-report expectations.

Leadership Expectations

The following list of leadership achievement expectations is the same for all leadership positions in all organizations at all management levels.

1. Customize expectations
2. Negotiate agreements
3. Cosign agreements
4. Conduct team achievement reviews
5. Determine causes of low achievement
6. Prepare improvement plans
7. Negotiate adverse personnel actions
8. Support achievement-based compensation
9. Interview and evaluate job applicants

Expectations one through six are the procedures for developing and executing partnering agreements. They are necessary for managers at all levels in all organizations. Expectations seven, eight, and nine are necessary but not assigned to all leaders. Number seven can be accomplished effectively by someone other than a direct report's leader. Number eight is best accomplished by a direct reports' leader, although most organizations don't have achievement based compensation programs in place. Number nine can be accomplished by someone other than the leader of a job for which an applicant is applying.

Leadership achievement expectations serve the following purposes:

- They define the leadership part of supervisors' jobs
- They are leadership learning activities
- They are leadership performance evaluation and performance improvement criteria

Achievement Expectations Compared

The left-hand column of the following list contains job duties drawn from a job description for a medical quality assurance program coordinator. The right-hand column illustrates a sample Achievement Expectation that corresponds to job duty four.

Job Description Job Duties	*Achievement Expectation Agreement for Job Duty Four*
1. Work with administration and medical director to insure comprehensive program delivery and quality patient care 2. Work with program heads to analyze, monitor, and ensure high levels of quality performance 3. Assist in development of goals and objectives for the quality assurance program 4. Explain quality assurance policies, procedures, systems, and objectives to staff 5. Research information from records and investigate areas of identified concern 6. Compute, analyze, and summarize data and present recommendations to management 7. Respond to requests for help in quality assurance troubleshooting	This organization is to be a leader in providing quality medical care to all people that we accept as recipients of our services. To accomplish this, all employees must understand and fully support our quality assurance objectives. I am responsible for assisting all leadership personnel in negotiating support commitments and excellent measurable quality achievement expectations with their direct reports. I am also responsible for making sure (1) that employees understand what support their direcct reports need to accomplish agreed-upon expectations, and (2) that leaders follow through with the support they have committed to direct reports or that leaders renegotiate expectations when they are unable to provide the support employees need to meet those expectations.

8. Participate in professional development efforts to ensure currency in quality assurance health care practices and trends
9. Attend required meetings
10. Perform related work

I will have demonstrated excellent achievement of this expectation when:

a. 90 % of all employees have partnering agreements that include excellent achievement targets.
b. 90 % of all quality-related expectations include excellent achievement targets.

Negotiated support: What specific support do I need from my leader in order to achieve these expectations? *A company policy that (1) requires all leaders to prepare, negotiate, and execute agreements with their direct reports; (2) requires me to review and approve the technical aspects of quality assurance expectations for all agreements; and (3) provides a budget for employee training when low achievement is caused by lack of knowledge or skill.*

The next list describes how job descriptions and partnering agreements differ in their approaches to human relations issues.

Job Descriptions	*Partnering Agreements*
Contain lists of employee duties (activities) void of support commitments	Contain leadership support expectations, leadership achievement expectations, and direct-report achievement expectations
Function as one-sided demand documents	Function as the foundation for synergistic work relationships
Are rarely prepared by the job holders' supervisors, thus void of supervisors' expectations	Are customized by leader–direct-report teams
Do not include leadership procedures	Include leadership procedures
Do not include empowering mechanisms	Include leaders' support commitments, which empower direct reports
Rarely foster satisfying supervisor-subordinate work relationships	Foster synergistic leader–direct-report relationships

Rarely personalize the corporate mission for individual employees	Personalize the corporate mission for each employee
Specify action descriptions that are not measurable	Specify objective measurable achievement expectations
Ask for subordinate sign-off that indicates only understanding of what job description says	Ask for employee sign-off that indicates understanding of expectations, leadership support, and the commitment to accomplish expectations as negotiated
Are one-sided supervisor judgments based on subjective guidelines	Compare actual achievement perceptions to agreed-upon achievement expectations
Ignore supervisory shortcomings and causes of low achievement	Compare actual support and achievement with committed support and achievement; target causes of low achievement
Are unclear as to purpose and value	Always support organizational missions and are always win-win
Review results unrelated to performance improvement programs such as Total Quality Management, customer service, performance-based compensation, and high-performance teams	Focus on causes of shortcomings, avoid blaming, and produce team improvement efforts to eliminate leader and direct-report shortcomings
Assume that employees are at fault for all low achievement and responsible for initiating all improvement efforts	Agree on one or two expectations to work on in order to improve team achievement; make change a team effort

Employee Partnering is Different from Current Practice

After going through these exercises and comparisons, you may think, "We are already doing most of those things." I hear this comment often, and I ask the following questions:

1. How do your company supervisors empower their employees to be partners with them?
2. What are some of the signed support commitments that your supervisors negotiate with their employees?
3. What are the written measurable achievement expectations that your supervisors negotiate with their employees?
4. How do your supervisors confirm that they are willing and able to support all of the achievement expectations they negotiate with their employees?

5. How do your company performance evaluations address low employee performance ratings that are caused by supervisory shortcomings?

Typically, answering question one focuses people's perception of empowerment. Their efforts to answer the question result in their convincing themselves that their employees were not as empowered as those employees needed to be.

Responses to question two reveal that some company supervisors do discuss the support that employees will need to accomplish expectations, but supervisors do not currently invite or empower employees to negotiate written supervisory commitments for employee support. Oral discussions of needed supervisory support are a big step in a positive direction. But leader–direct-report team's negotiated and documented specific support items for each achievement expectation are a giant step ahead of undocumented, unguided discussion.

Some responses to question three describe systems that are similar to employee partnering expectations with the exception of the most important part. Currently company supervisors do not negotiate expectations that include objective and measurable achievement descriptions. But it is these agreed-upon measures of success that allow supervisors and employees to negotiate mutual understanding of and deep commitment to expectations.

Answers to question four show that the questioners' companies do not have a system in which supervisors negotiate the support they will provide for each employee expectation. Yet this is the only procedure that causes supervisors to be proactive in employee support. It is the only way to make sure that employees have a reasonable opportunity to achieve that which supervisors expect.

People's responses to question five reveal that people often recognize that management may contribute to employee performance problems. Some organizations even have some form of supervisory performance evaluation. However, even these organizations do not use employee performance evaluations that pinpoint the actual causes of performance deficiencies, including supervisory shortcomings. Nor do their employee performance improvement plans include supervisory performance improvement efforts, yet these efforts are essential when supervisory shortcomings cause employee deficiencies.

Typical discussions of these questions illustrate that partnering with employees is not what companies already do, nor is it just another management program. Moreover, partnering does not require many committee meetings to decide what to do. The implementation time required is only about twenty-five hours per employee, over a period of about six weeks. And finally, this book is the ready-made implementation tool for human relations professionals and enlightened managers to use.

Based on my experience with clients, partnering makes ordinary improvement efforts up to seventy times more productive. Work nurtures people as well as compensates them. Supervisors become leaders, sharing their power and having more influence and success. Customer satisfaction and profits increase in proportion to job satisfaction, not at the expense of it. The following sections describe factors that inhibit ordinary efforts to improve human relations performance. The second paragraph of each section explains how partnering can make ordinary improvement efforts seventy times more productive. This supporting information is based on my research cited in the Preface.

Improvement Efforts Directed at the Wrong Causes

About 89 percent of persistent low achievement is caused by a lack of employee understanding or leadership support. Supervisors are the source of expectations and support. Yet most improvement remedies are based on the assumption that employees are responsible for initiating improvement efforts.

Partnering agreements ensure that both leaders and direct reports understand expectation and support commitments. The agreements also empower reports to safely and successfully discuss problems with leaders and to negotiate win-win resolutions when the employees do not sufficiently understand expectations or have enough support.

Wrong Kind of Improvement Effort Chosen

The lack of knowledge or skill causes only 10 percent of persistent supervisory performance deficiencies. Yet training and education are the remedies of choice in nearly all efforts to improve supervisory performance.

Partnering performance evaluation discussions pinpoint the actual causes of performance deficiencies. Leader-direct-report teams structure their improvement efforts to eliminate specific mutually agreed-upon causes. Training and education are applied only to shortcomings caused by the lack of knowledge or skill.

Employees Do Not Apply What They Learn

Supervisors rarely discuss their employee achievement expectations with their employees. As a result, employees rarely understand when, why, or how their achievement is deficient. They have no basis on which to determine relevant performance improvement needs or to apply any new capabilities they have gained.

Because partnering makes achievement expectations clear, it makes shortcomings and their causes clear. Leader-direct-report teams can make improvement plans that actually produce expected achievement increases because the plans include remedies specifically selected to eliminate the agreed-upon causes of deficiencies. As a result, direct reports have a vehicle for applying their new skills and knowledge. They know when, why, and how to use what they learn.

Hostile Win-Lose Work Cultures Exist

The three preceding factors are trademarks of win-lose cultures. These cultures prevent employees from knowing what to improve or how to improve and, thus, how to change these cultures. In these self-perpetuating win-lose cultures, continuous improvement is only wishful thinking.

Employee partnering is the tool that can change these conditions. It creates win-win cultures that support and sustain continuous improvement for all participating employees.

Using Partnering with Existing Improvement Programs

The following performance improvement programs have the potential to produce far greater benefits than they have in the past. This potential is realized when these programs are used to remedy specific deficiencies as part of an employee partnering program. The following information describes how partnering can support each existing program.

Achievement-based compensation programs. Performance-based compensation programs grounded on ordinary performance evaluations follow win-lose procedures that create distrust and animosity and decrease productivity. Partnering agreements develop trust between leaders and direct reports so that achievement evaluation results can support fair achievement-based compensation without compromising relationships or performance improvement.

ADA (Americans with Disabilities Act) programs. Partnering agreements provide definitions of performance expectations for hiring, inspiring, supporting, and compensating workers with disabilities so that both employers and disabled job applicants can clearly relate worker capabilities to achievement expectations. Most job descriptions fail to specify expectations as a basis for disabled applicants to assess their capability in relation to job demands.

Assessment and benchmarking programs. Benchmarking means setting standards by which to compare other, similar kinds of performance. Such programs often suffer because the standards set are arbitrary. Negotiated achievement expectations are benchmarks developed by leaders and direct reports to serve as bases for accurate achievement assessments and to support continuous performance improvement.

Communication programs. Most communication programs teach people skills but don't help them apply the skills. Partnering agreements provide procedures that ensure complete, productive, and mutually satisfying exchanges of information, perceptions, and expectations between leaders, direct reports, and all other stakeholders.

Employee involvement programs. Partnering is total employee involvement. Partnering agreements cannot be negotiated and implemented without creating true employee involvement.

Empowerment programs. Most empowerment programs teach people about the subject but cannot cause empowerment to happen, no matter how much people learn about the subject. Partnering agreements empower employees by putting them in control of what they agree to when they negotiate expectations, negotiate support to accomplish expectations, evaluate achievement, and design performance improvement plans.

Job enrichment programs. Partnering agreements produce employee commitment to worthwhile achievement expectations. Partnering also produces the leadership support that insures job success and satisfaction. It supports employees in their efforts to expand their jobs and apply creative twists to what they do, and encourages them to take more risks in the pursuit of personal growth and increased production for their employer.

Leadership development programs. Most leadership training does not change the work culture that inhibits people from implementing what they learn. Leadership achievement expectations in partnering agreements define leadership procedures, guide leaders in performing the procedures, create supportive work cultures, and effect continuous improvement in leadership performance.

Motivational programs. Most motivation programs serve to increase supervisors' ability to manipulate employees. Partnering agreements produce leader and direct-report commitment to clearly defined areas of responsibility, levels of achievement, and support, which generates self-fulfillment and self-motivation. Partnering procedures create the conditions under which employees motivate themselves.

Organizational development programs. The mission of organizational professionals is to implement processes that improve the effectiveness of organizations. They typically apply training as the means to accomplish change in organizations. Organizations change very little as a direct result of training. They only change significantly when as a group and as individuals they develop a vision and a mission and are committed to both. Partnering causes organizations and individuals to clarify their vision and mission and personalizes vision and mission for individuals. Organizational development needs are incorporated into every employee's partnering agreement. Partnering is organizational development.

Performance evaluation programs. Ordinary performance reviews commonly create animosity and distrust and stifle productivity. They don't address supervisor-caused employee performance problems. Partnering performance reviews compare leader–direct-report perceptions of achievement in a win-win manner that employees enjoy. Both leaders and reports determine the specific causes of low achievement and together design the performance improvement that will eliminate the causes.

Problem-solving programs. Typical problem-solving programs develop problem-solving skills but, like leadership training, they don't change the work culture that inhibits employee involvement and good problem-solving activity. Partnering agreements empower employees to be creative and resourceful in preventing and solving problems. Partnering also creates conditions in which leaders and direct reports regularly take action to prevent problems as well as to solve them.

Programs to eliminate sexual harassment, discrimination, and other causes of grievance. Partnering agreements ensure that managers are up front, unbiased, and fair in their expectations and support and that expectations and support are formally documented. Leaders accept responsibility for their own shortcomings in leader–direct-report relationships. Leadership or direct-report behavior that is a problem to others is addressed in performance improvement plans to remedy them.

Programs to reduce span of control. Partnering agreements reduce the need for supervision. They produce employees who are empowered, who understand expectations, who are self-motivated to prevent and solve problems, and who are self-reliant.

Team-building programs. Ordinary team-building programs ignore the basic team (leader–direct-report). Yet relationships between leaders and direct reports affect the way people participate on other teams. Partnering agreements produce leader–direct-report team relationships that support synergistic participation on all other organization teams by both leaders and reports.

Total Quality Management programs. Partnering agreements translate every aspect of Total Quality Management philosophy and specific performance requirements into individual employee achievement expectations. Just as a computer's disk-operating system makes all the other software perform correctly, partnering creates the conditions under which all performance improvement programs operate effectively.

The positive influences of partnering described in this section are synergistic; each energizes all the others so that the total influence is more than the sum of the individual benefits. Win-win relationships encourage people to discover their deficiencies and correct them. Leaders support this discovery process, rather than hinder it. People understand and agree upon what is expected of them and what they need to do to achieve expectations. People design improvement remedies that are always appropriate to the causes of performance shortcomings. Employees apply most of what they learn because this application is necessary to achieve commitments. The combined effect of these positive influences makes improvement efforts usually seventy times more productive.

2

The Essential Elements of Successful Partnering

A main goal of this book is to guide leader-direct-report teams, in any size or kind of organization, to synergistic, fulfilling, and profitable relationships. The principles in this chapter are the philosophical basis of a nurturing and productive leadership style rather than a dominating win-lose style. While the first style is sometimes associated with a feminine or matriarchal outlook and the second style with a masculine or patriarchal viewpoint, I believe that the nurturing and productive style can be used effectively and comfortably by everyone, because its results are so positive for all relationships and organizations. By following these principles, leaders inspire, guide, and support efforts to set and accomplish goals that far exceed the goals achievable through individual production efforts.

Integrity

Of all the principles that make human interactions satisfying and productive, integrity is the one with which there can be no compromise. It has to be the most certain and the least subject to doubt of all human qualities, and it may be the one that most affects people's feelings about each other and their work relationships. People tend to project their feelings about themselves onto others. Trustworthy leaders make positive assumptions about direct reports and expect them to act with integrity. When leaders are trustworthy, direct reports usually reciprocate with similar behavior.

Integrity Is More Than Not Lying

Leaders' integrity shows when they demonstrate complete understanding of their expectations and ask direct reports to accomplish no more than the leaders have committed to support. Leaders show lack of integrity when they ask direct reports to commit to accomplishments that the leaders do not fully commit to support.

Many years ago, I attended two seminars on effective delegation that taught participants how to get tasks off their backs and onto someone else's. The principle was to assign tasks to the lowest-paid people who were capable of accomplishing them, thus freeing the higher-paid people to use their higher-priced time on more complicated problems.

The principle seemed logical at the time, but in retrospect, I realized that no consideration was given to those to whom tasks were delegated (or, more accurately, to those who were dumped on). Nothing was ever said in those seminars about asking people what support they might need to accomplish the delegated assignments. This oversight explains why the delegation process is all too often win-lose.

Another example of failed integrity was the company president who expected his project managers to supervise company superintendents but refused to give the managers authority to make the decisions necessary to answer the superintendents' urgent questions. For that reason, the superintendents ignored the project managers as leaders. The owner's refusal to support his own expectations for the project managers blocked the growth of the company until the project managers were empowered to accomplish those expectations.

Leaders show integrity when they set the example for performance that they expect of others. In addition to setting examples by what they do, they set examples by what they enforce. At one time, a friend of mine owned a large construction company. Joe felt strongly about his company's image, and his policy was that no unsafe or dirty equipment was to leave the equipment compound. One day, he saw a muddy company crane on the street two blocks from the compound. Flagging the crane to a stop, he asked the driver where he was going with the dirty machine. The driver told him that another company crane had broken down and that no one on that project could do anything until they had a replacement.

Fully aware that what he was about to say would cost his company over $1,000, Joe asked, "Do you know the company policy that nothing leaves the yard unsafe or looking bad?"

The driver said he did but repeated, "Nothing is happening on the project until I get there with this."

Joe replied, "So the quicker you get this machine washed, the quicker things will get going again on the project." Joe's consistency made his integrity legendary in his company and a model that most employees liked to uphold.

Integrity Is Supporting Direct Reports

A leader's understanding of and respect for human rights also demonstrates integrity. Any time a person with power uses it at the expense of others, the immediate results are win-lose. However, when employees are abused or injured in any way, they cannot be optimally productive, so in the long term, everyone who has a stake in the organization loses.

Leaders' respect for human rights shows up in the way they represent direct reports' interests in reports' absence. Do leaders support their reports when the leaders are under pressure on reports' behalf, or do leaders use the reports as scapegoats, to take pressure off the leaders? In the long term, putting direct reports' interests first is beneficial to everyone.

I experienced this truth with a very bright, ebullient, assertive young black woman who was hired as my secretary. Karen and I were responsible to a board of trustees in our work on the Construction Advancement Program. After five years, she was doing the work of a program director, which commonly paid $30,000 to $32,000 per year. Her annual salary at the time was $21,500.

When Karen and I discussed my recommending her for promotion to program director, she suggested and I agreed to a request for a salary of $29,500. I told her I would support her request but couldn't "guarantee" it. Karen said she had "trust" that I would accomplish what was right.

In an initial budget meeting, which lacked a quorum, the trustees approved Karen's promotion, but at a salary of only $26,000 per year. Their rationale was that a 21 percent increase was a big raise. I tried unsuccessfully to convince them that the issue was a promotion with a commensurate salary, not simply a raise.

On hearing the initial results, Karen acted disappointed but not devastated. I also explained that there was still a chance for success at a future meeting when a quorum was present and final action could be taken. However, at the next session, the discussion evolved exactly as it had previously. The 21 percent raise was passed unanimously, and the chairman adjourned the meeting. Then a simple solution jumped out at me. Before the trustees were out of earshot, I blurted out, "Just so you don't find out through the grapevine, I want you all to know that I'm going to take the $3,500 raise that you approved for me and add it to the $26,000 that you approved for Karen. It is more important that she gets what is right and deserving than it is for me to have that raise."

The trustees all returned, sat down, rescinded the previous motion, approved the promotion and the $29,500 salary, and made no mention of my raise. I was dumbfounded. Each of them thanked me for my integrity and persistence. My spontaneous tangible support for Karen had communicated what my rational persuasion had not. Because of it, the trustees finally understood the importance of the issues on which they had debated.

The trustees' action elated Karen, but it didn't surprise her. She truly had trusted me, and she went on to outstanding achievements. The trustees were rewarded for their decision both in the value of Karen's services and in the new level of respect that they felt for her and her position.

Integrity Is Owning Your Own Problems

Another act of integrity is taking ownership of one's responsibilities for relationship problems. In adversarial relationships, differences cause problems, especially differences that one person perceives as the other person's shortcomings. When confronted with differences, people are inclined to think that those who are believed to have caused the problems should confess the error of their ways and change their behavior to meet others' expectations. This ineffective kind of problem solving results in supervisors and subordinates each waiting for the other to admit error and volunteer to improve. Such an approach produces much waiting and much frustration, but little productive change.

A rule of thumb in building relationships is that people cannot force others to change. What they can do is change the way they respond to others' behavior. They can accept ownership of their discomfort about differences with others. They can understand that the problem that can be solved belongs to them, not to the others. The act of admitting ownership of the discomfort puts the problem under the owner's control. It empowers the owner to initiate solutions to relationship problems.

An example of taking ownership of problems to resolve differences is my experience with a boss who was constantly cantankerous and aloof when he was in the office, but who was often absent without reason from the office. The only staff person he talked to freely during that time was the female bookkeeper, and his behavior was causing untold obstacles to the entire staff's ability to perform.

One day, in a staff meeting, I persistently questioned something the boss said. He became very defensive and stopped the meeting. After that he avoided me and refused to schedule regular staff meetings. When he did call a meeting, six weeks later, I saw it as a chance for me, my co-workers—Dave, Charles, and Kay—and the boss to discuss our staff relationship problems. Dave, Charles, Kay, and I met ahead of time to plan our strategy. We agreed that the only way our boss would listen to any of us was for the four of us to speak as one voice. That would give us protection, power, and credibility. We also did not want to accuse him of causing problems and thus increase his defensiveness. We viewed our concerns as our own problems and talked about them as issues with which we needed his help. Accepting ownership was a bit of a stretch for two of us, but it was essential for all of us to do it.

Each of us agreed to lead a discussion on two of the issues about which we were most concerned. We planned the sequence in which each of us would bring up our issues, but we didn't want to appear rehearsed, so we had cues to signal when the next person was to take the lead.

We expected there would be a few minutes of banter when the meeting started. The anticipated cue for me to kick off the plan was the point at which the boss began the meeting agenda. When that cue came at the actual meeting, I asked the boss to consider a work problem issue first. He growled, "If this is to be a repeat of last time, I don't think I want to discuss any of your problems!" As we had planned, I then apologized for not having communicated what I had intended the previous time and for causing him discomfort. I assured him that I needed his help, but said nothing about his behavior. His defensive demeanor drained away, his face gradually relaxed, he slouched back into his chair, and said, "Okay, what's this about?"

Dave jumped into action. He is a nonstop talker, but he hates confrontation. So we thought that having him lead off with his first concern would hook the boss's interest. Dave was sweating and dry mouthed, but his performance was magnificent. His comments were to the point and had the perfect effect. The group trust building was quick and rewarding.

The boss responded better than we had hoped. He listened and offered positive suggestions. The rest of us commented when we had something to add. When Dave had satisfied his concern, he confirmed it to all of us and thanked the boss and the rest of us for the useful and satisfying exchange. On cue, each of us lead a discussion on our first issue. All of the exchanges went very smoothly with similar results and satisfaction.

The trust was such that, in the second round, Charles showed little anxiety explaining how he had resorted to leaking comments to the bookkeeper in order to communicate with the boss. The boss even agreed that Charles's clandestine method had worked. It took only two hours and five minutes to resolve all eight of our concerns, and the four of us were elated with the overall results. In addition, the boss ended his social relationship with the bookkeeper. Later the boss thanked me, saying that the four of us had helped him get his life "back in order." He said that the discussion was one of the "most painful but rewarding experiences" in his life. He scheduled regular staff meetings again, office staff ceased griping and gossiping, and we all marveled at how productive working conditions had become.

The key to the solution had been our acceptance of ownership for the problems we had perceived. The four of us were 80 percent of the organization's professional staff. We worked out our own differences and created a resolute team objective and strategy during our planning meeting. Through those efforts we had more practical power in the meeting with our boss than he did and we led every step in that part of the meeting. But the root of our our success was our integrity and our win-win motive, not our power. Our strategy and actions were consistent with our motive—the essence of partnering with employees.

Teamwork Reflects Leader–Direct-Report Relationships

A team is a number of individuals associated in cooperative action. Entire organizations are teams; divisions and departments within organizations are also teams. Work crews, quality circles, project groups, committees, and associations are all teams. The level of a team's performance always depends on the working relationships between individual leaders and direct reports. Without win-win relationships between teams of leaders and direct reports, teamwork at other levels is severely handicapped.

Team building is a hot topic on organizations' lists for education and training programs. Organizations also feel a growing urgency for all employees to cooperate more with each other within the total organizational team. However, in most organizations, the concern over team training puts the cart in front of the horse. The demand for better teamwork comes about because the work culture inhibits change and stymies team building for any purpose. Training cannot solve this cultural problem. The solution starts with changing win-lose supervisor-subordinate team relationships to win-win leader-direct-report relationships.

Leader-Direct-Report Teams

The basic team in any organization is the leader and the direct report. The value of employee participation on all other teams reflects direct reports' relationships with leaders. Partnering agreements establish and nurture these basic leader-direct-report team relationships.

Most teams are organized to accomplish a special mission, and this mission influences each team's make-up. By comparison, all leader-direct-report teams have a common mission, which is to cooperate in determining the team's part in the organizations' overall mission and to work to accomplish that part.

Figure 2.1 represents leader-direct-report teams as a part of larger teams. The A, B, and C levels together depict a typical organization team. The A and B levels and the B and C levels show typical leader-direct-report teams. The single lines represent the traditional flow of official communication up and down the hierarchy. The double lines represent employee partnering agreements. The teams-within-teams concept applies to organizations of any number of management levels.

All persons in all organizations, except the top executives, are direct reports in at least one leader-direct-report team. Many are members of two or more

Figure 2.1. Typical Leader-Direct-Report Teams.

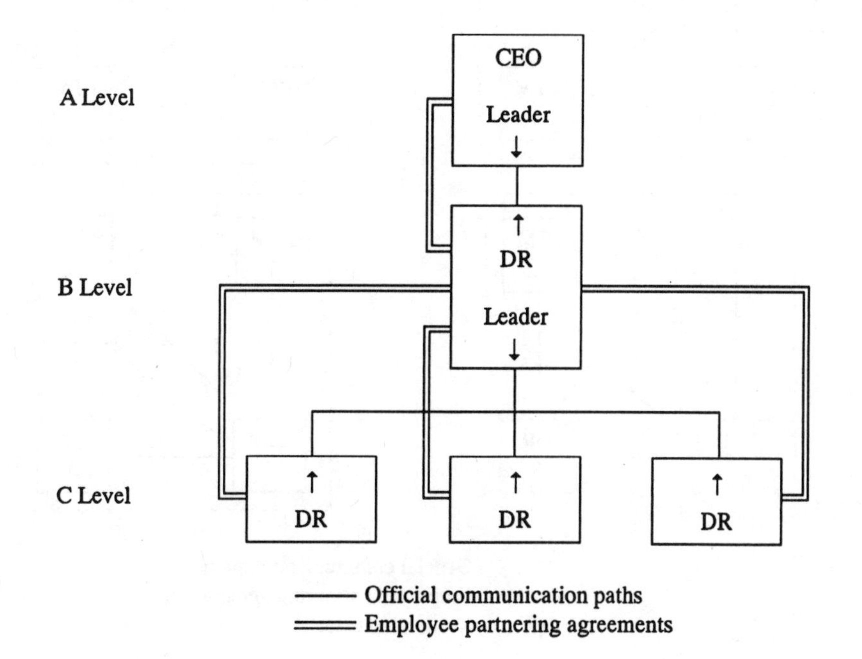

leader-direct-report teams at one time. The person at the B level of Fig. 2.1 is a leader on three leader-direct-report teams and a direct report on a fourth. Partnering agreements define all these leader-direct-report teams and guide their relationships.

Self-Managed Teams

The leader of a leader-direct-report team can be a team. In a family, for example, parents may act as a team in some of their relationships with their children. Some organizations operate with work teams that have no individually assigned leaders; they are self-managed. Such teams assign work, conduct performance evaluations, and recommend raises. The team itself functions as the leader with individual team members reporting to the team as a whole.

Leader-direct-report teams work well with more than one person operating as the leader when all those who form the leadership team within the team have agreed to one set of expectations for each team member. It is common for direct reports to work concurrently for more than one leader or to change leaders frequently. Construction workers regularly rotate to different foremen. Figure 2.2

Figure 2.2. Self-Managed Team.

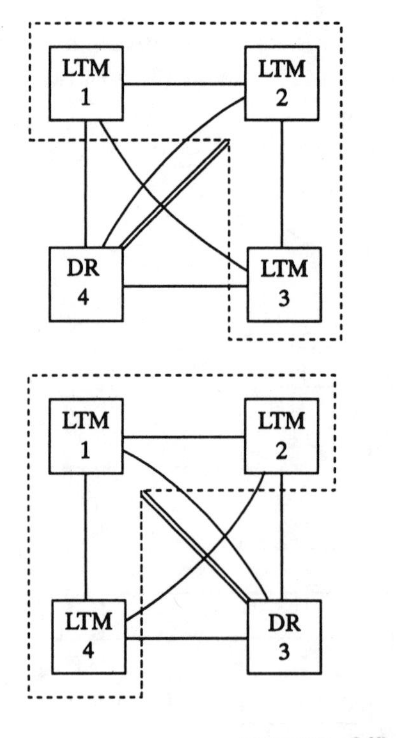

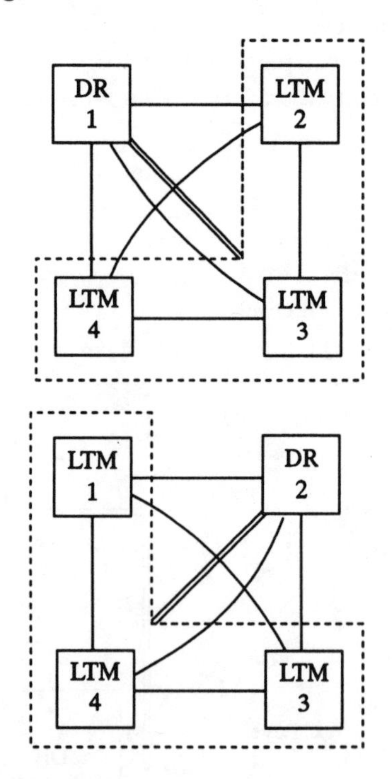

Official communication paths
Employee partnering agreements
Leadership team

illustrates how individuals' roles shift from leadership team member (LTM) to direct report (DR) on a four-member self-managed team.

The leadership groups (enclosed in dashed lines) operate with one set of negotiated expectations for each individual. This way, one or more leadership team members can represent the leadership team in transactions with individual team members. Each person is a direct report to the leadership team and each person is part of the leadership team.

Teams in a Matrix

Figure 2.3 illustrates a third structure in which official communication lines connect not only the leader and each direct report but also connect all the direct reports to each other. All members may contribute to each other's performance reviews, but the leader has the final responsibility for decisions. Regardless of management structure, leader-direct-report teams are fundamental to all organizations.

Employee Involvement

The potential that team members will have for synergistic relationships depends on each member's self-confidence and involvement in team interactions. This is especially true in leader-direct-report teams. Employee involvement is a partner-

Figure 2.3. Leader-Direct-Report Teams in a Matrix.

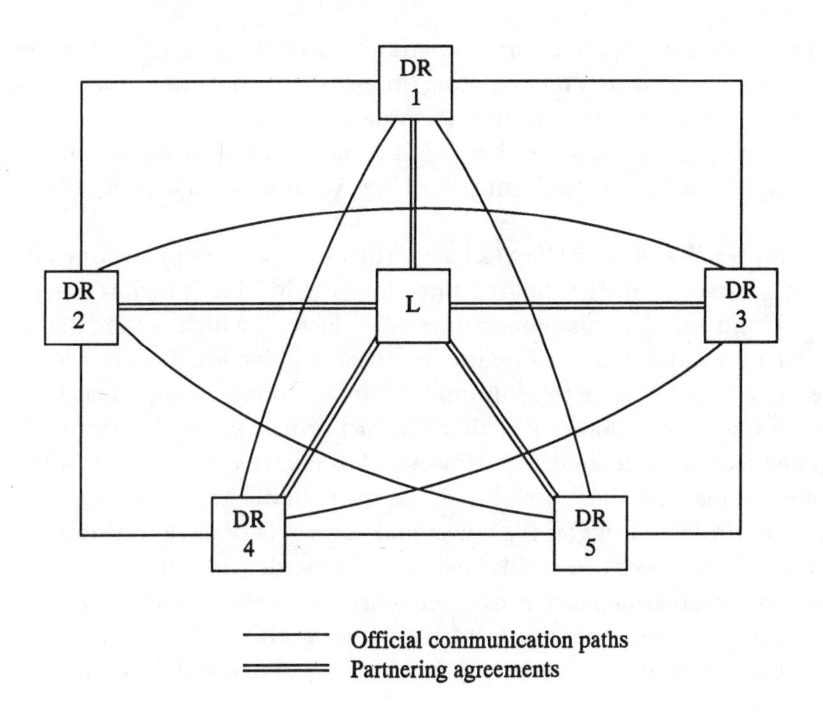

ing principle that depends on leaders' making direct reports feel like partners in the team's transactions. Direct reports can act as partners only when they are empowered and have a feeling of self-worth.

Self-Worth

Self-worth is a person's perception of his or her own value. Individuals gain self-worth when they accomplish anything that is worthwhile to themselves and to others for whom they have respect. The amount of effort individuals expend and the self-discipline they exercise determine the self-worth that they gain from their accomplishments. Individuals can develop self-worth by intentionally setting worthwhile goals, committing to the goals, and achieving them. Partnering agreements ensure that leaders and direct reports gain self-worth from their jobs.

Abraham Maslow (1968) discusses six needs that every individual seeks progressively to satisfy. Activities that address the last three of these needs produce feelings of self-worth in individuals and cause them to be synergistic team members. The list begins with the most basic needs and moves to the highest needs. Typically, individuals address the basic needs first.

1. Physical needs are air, water, food, warmth, rest, sex, sleep, and shelter.
2. Security needs are a safe and stable environment, continuous employment, adequate salary or wages, fringe benefits, a position in a pecking order, and protection of self, property, and reputation.
3. Social needs are having interaction with others, being understood, and feeling loved.
4. Intellectual needs are informational, understanding subjects of interest, discovering new ideas, and exploring and solving problems.
5. Ego needs are respect, prestige, status, and power.
6. Self-fulfillment needs are freedom of choice, the fullest use of one's capabilities, self-sufficiency, and interdependency, rather than dependency.

Frederick Herzberg (1968) added further observations to Maslow's findings. Herzberg determined that the first three levels of Maslow's hierarchy—physical, security, and social needs—are maintenance factors, which means that individuals have to satisfy them to maintain reasonable health. Employers help employees satisfy these needs through compensation, fringe benefits, safety programs, working conditions, labor contract provisions, and personnel policies designed to address these needs. However, leaders have little direct influence on employees' meeting these three needs, because maintenance needs are rarely affected by win-lose struggles for power and control between supervisors and subordinates. Employees can satisfy maintenance needs without being empowered. They can meet maintenance needs even when they are controlled.

Jobs and work relationships that satisfy nothing more than maintenance needs cause individuals to show up for work regularly and do what supervisors demand. That is, maintenance needs typically cause individuals to accomplish a maintenance level of achievement. Satisfying only these physical, security, and social needs rarely causes individuals to gain in self-worth, enjoy their work, accomplish excellence, or continuously improve their capability. Herzberg called the maintenance needs *dissatisfiers,* because they produce more action when they are not met than when they are met. When maintenance needs go unmet, employees often rebel. It was unmet maintenance needs that gave birth to unions.

Herzberg also concluded that intellectual, ego, and self-fulfillment requirements are true motivating factors—sources of real satisfaction. They are not necessary to maintain normal physical health, so Herzberg prefers to call them *desires* or *satisfiers.* Job-related ego, intellectual, and self-fulfillment satisfaction arise as a result of employees' being partners in their work relationships and in the decisions related to their jobs. People gain self-worth in proportion to the amount of control they have over their jobs. Partnering produces satisfaction and self-worth and therefore motivates achievement above a maintenance level.

Figure 2.4 is a graphic representation of the combined concepts. The vertical axis represents tension and the horizontal axis represents self-worth. When the tension of a factor peaks, it gets attention. When people act to relieve the tension caused by a lack of satisfaction with five of the six needs and desires, the tension from those sources drops off. However, no needs and desires ever go away completely. They all remain ready to rise again when they are not met.

Physical needs are the most basic needs on which people act to relieve tension. As individuals satisfy physical tensions, these tensions diminish and security tensions peak. Tension rises for each succeeding factor as the previous one is satisfied. As Figure 2.4 illustrates, when one tension has peaked and dropped off, the succeeding tension will drop less: Individuals maintain more appetite for each successive need or desire. The desire for self-fulfillment is the last to peak, and it does not drop off. Individuals never get enough of self-

Figure 2.4. Hierarchy of Human Needs and Desires.

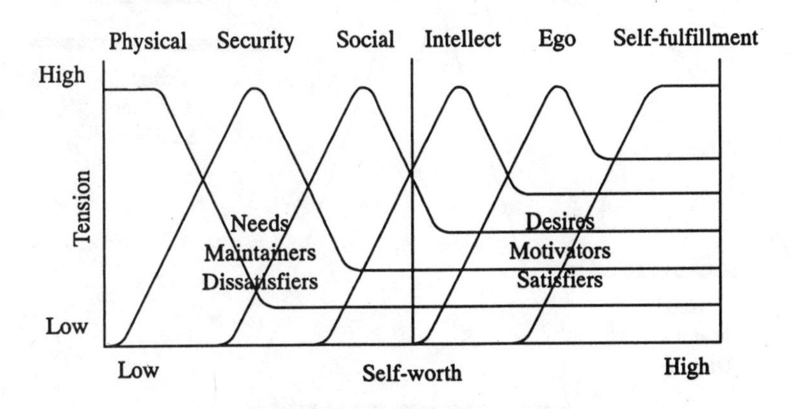

Source: Adapted from Graduate School of Agriculture, 1971.

fulfillment. It never diminishes as a motivator. This insatiable need underlies the adage, "Success begets success." The self-fulfillment curve shows personal achievement's unique ability to produce self-worth and self motivation.

Balance

Figure 2.5 graphically represents the way many people feel about their work experience. Weighted down on the maintenance side, the scale depicts lives that are out of balance and in despair due to the preponderance in their lives of maintainers relative to motivators. The tipped scale reflects the way employees feel when they are not in control of their jobs.

Labor contract settlements, human rights laws, worker protection laws, and other worker gains, have added much to the left side of the scale in the last fifty years. Very little has been added to the right side. The gains in physical well-being and reduced dissatisfaction are important, but few contribute to satisfaction and to worthwhile accomplishments. Fulfilled maintenance needs do practically nothing to reduce the controlling nature of supervision in win-lose cultures. In fact, some of the maintenance need gains have been offered as trade-offs, so that organizations can gain more control over employees' behavior.

The more individuals are controlled, the less they are in control and the more stress they feel in work relationships and in their lives. Not knowing the true cause of the stress, individuals and groups seek to relieve their imbalance

Figure 2.5. Employees' Common Mental State.

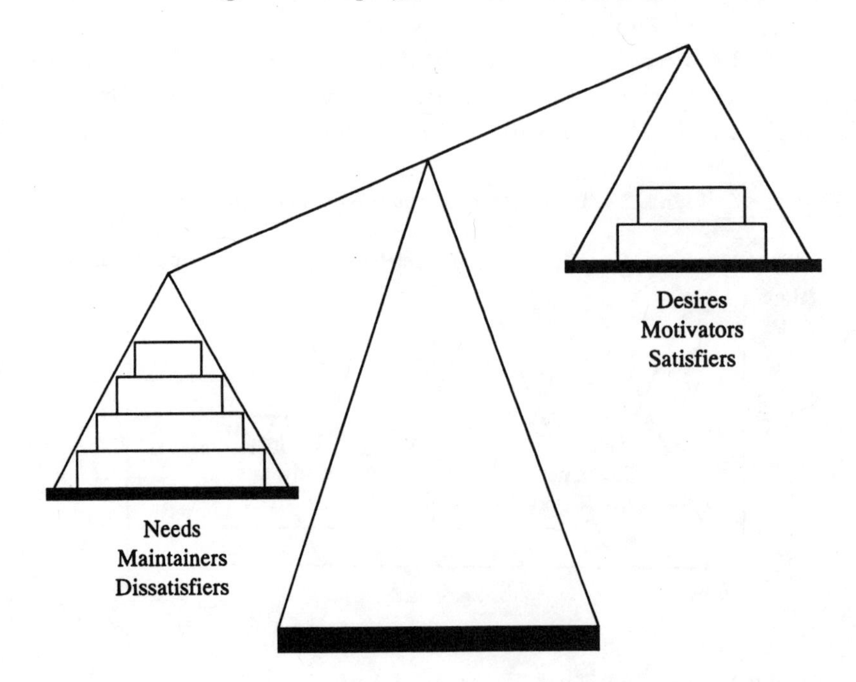

discomfort by pushing for more maintenance gains. They seek more compensation and special parking spaces, treatment, and office furniture; they ask for extra time off, special titles and privileges, and various other perks. None of these gains puts individuals in control of their jobs or relieves the tension and emptiness they feel from lack of self-worth.

Adding more maintenance items without a corresponding balance of satisfiers is more problematic than beneficial. It increases the imbalance (stress) between maintainers and motivators, making people feel worse rather than better. The situation is analogous to drinking coffee to get relief from insomnia.

The solution to this imbalance calls for individuals to be in control of their jobs and achieve success. When employees are empowered in relation to their jobs, they make commitments to worthwhile accomplishments and achieve them. Leaders help direct reports accomplish this by providing worthwhile and realistic expectations and the support that direct reports need to achieve their commitments.

The way partnering agreements generate self-worth is illustrated by the following story about a boy who did poorly in school. For ten years, his mother reported, she and his father "cajoled, bribed, and threatened him." Nothing happened until they enrolled him in an alternative high school, where the teachers and students negotiated contracts for specific, measurable student achievement and for teacher support. The boy became "a different person." He acted responsible, earned good grades, and got along much better with everyone. His mother is convinced that "his turnaround is all because he helps decide what is worthwhile for him and he gets a lot of satisfaction out of surpassing his achievement commitments."

Charles Coonradt and Lee Nelson (1985) give another example of the positive value of leaders' helping employees make measurable commitments and supporting their achievement. Coonradt and Nelson were asked to help a package express company file their millions of freight bills more efficiently. Working on the principle that "if you can't measure it, you can't manage it," they and a company vice president devised a system of weighing the material to be filed (each freight bill was the same weight) as a measure of how much was filed each day. According to Coonradt and Nelson,

> The first week we came up with an average of twenty-two ounces per person-hour. We didn't really know if that was good or bad, but it was a start. The next week we developed a scorecard for the workers and taught them how to keep score as if we were teaching them a game. They recorded their own ounces per person-hours.
>
> An interesting thing happened. The group average for the second week increased to thirty-three ounces per person-hour. And by the end of that week they were only one day behind—the first time in thirty-six years. We were witnessing a miracle.
>
> The supervisor came to me and said, "Listen, I can't go any faster and be accurate."

> "I understand that. That's all right. Don't worry about it."
>
> The next week production increased to forty-five ounces per person-hour. There was no monetary incentive, no threatened disciplinary measures, no promised promotions. The only difference was that they were measuring performance, keeping score. Not only was the department no longer behind, but they were finishing each day's filing by 2 P.M. By the fourth week, production had increased to fifty-four ounces per person-hour and filing was finished each day by 11:30 A.M.
>
> I remembered when the supervisor was doing twenty-two ounces per hour and telling me she couldn't go any faster. The last time I checked she was up to seventy-two ounces per hour and still increasing.
>
> The big payoff was that the four people doing the filing were part of an eight-person work force in that department. When two of the non-file clerks needed to quit, the file clerks came to their supervisor and said, "Listen, if you'll tell us how to measure what they've been doing, we'll just pick it up [p. 40].

Illusion of Employee Involvement

There is a common misunderstanding about employee involvement. Many supervisors believe that they are practicing employee involvement when they ask employees to prepare their own job descriptions, work plans, or production objectives. However, the request is usually devoid of any clear supervisory expectations, and an invitation to write one's own job description without knowing the formal job expectations is like fool's gold—common metal that only looks like gold and that produces more disappointment than satisfaction.

Under these circumstances, employees cannot determine the value or relevance of their ideas to their organizations' mission. When employees accede to this request, they are at risk of expecting too much or too little, of failing to perform as their offerings specify, and of being blamed for supervisory shortcomings. The job description process perpetuates their being controlled and prevents their supervisors from functioning as leaders. In this false employee involvement, supervisors sit in judgment and react to employees' offerings. Without documented negotiated expectations for employee achievement, supervisors react to employees' job descriptions using their personal attitudes, habits, and biases as their only criteria. As a result, supervisors tend to reject anything that is not consistent with their own biases. No matter what employees come up with, this process does not put them in control. Moreover, putting employees at risk this way produces grievances, mistrust, and acts of sabotage that are the opposite of the actions and feelings that create self-worth. The results confuse, frustrate, and hurt employees. It is a rude awakening for proponents of this process when employees feel miserable rather than satisfied after participating in this false employee involvement.

True employee involvement results from the preparation and execution of employee partnering agreements. Organizational missions dictate what leaders and direct reports need to accomplish. Leaders interpret their organizations' missions. They individualize missions for their direct reports and negotiate partnering agreements to achieve these missions through clear achievement and support expectations. True employee involvement is continuous and generates extraordinary achievement and mutual feelings of self-worth.

3

Shifting the Basis of Work Relationships

This chapter describes the principles that produce effective and mutually satisfying negotiations. Discussions that adhere to these principles usually accomplish win-win results.

Mutual Expectations

Mutual expectations are the heart of leader–direct-report relationships and of employee partnering agreements. Ideally, leaders expect excellent achievement from direct reports for their job areas of responsibility. Ideally, direct reports want to understand leaders' expectations for them and to have the support needed to accomplish the expectations. Expectations are the means by which leaders create visions and generate energy. Through expectations, they inspire their direct reports to succeed and gain feelings of self-worth. Leaders' commitments to provide support are the source of direct reports' empowerment, creativity, perseverance, and fulfillment.

Many supervisors communicate expectations to employees, but the expectations are seldom objective, clear, or measurable. They give employees no basis on which to judge their own accomplishments or guide improvement of their own performances. Even formal job descriptions rarely define a level of accomplishment that supervisors and employees can mutually understand. Instead, job descriptions and other forms of employee performance plans usually function as unilateral demands for activity rather than achievement.

When I asked a group of professional secretaries who received regular performance reviews how many of them believed their reviews were based on their job descriptions or other performance criteria, all agreed that their evaluations were not based on performance criteria specific to their jobs. The secretaries expected to be rated on how their work pleased their bosses and to be told when their bosses were not happy with what the secretaries did. Nothing in the secretaries' responses hinted of mutual expectations. Instead the secretaries appeared totally dependent on supervisors to control their work lives.

A lack of supervisory support commitments allows and encourages supervisors to make unfair and even illegal assignments. Furthermore, even when supervisors' expectations are specific and measurable, they are ordinarily production objectives. It is simple to recognize whether an employee has met a production objective. However, knowledge that employees achieved or failed to achieve production objectives is rarely useful. It does not pinpoint the deficient behavior that employees need to understand in order to improve. This is the basic reason Management by Objectives rarely produces individual performance improvement. Reviewing the results of their production objectives rarely does more than cause people to feel good when they accomplish the objectives, and bad when they do not.

Partnering expectations define achievement that is desired as a direct result of employee performance. They make it simple to pinpoint performance that needs improving, to identify causes of low achievement, and to structure performance remedies. These abilities are essential to continuous performance improvement.

As with other parts of this system, I perfected the process of documenting mutual expectations in my own work experience before I recognized it as part of partnering. A director I once worked for was a perfectionist and a demanding but fair leader, but he was not always easy to understand. Yet I admired and respected him so much that when we discussed mutual expectations, I always made certain that when we finished our conversation he and I were united in our understanding of what we had agreed to. Although I knew it was his responsibility to ensure that I understood him, I assumed that responsibility myself. I always took good notes and before we parted, I would describe what I planned to accomplish and when it would be accomplished. If I expected to need anything that I couldn't get on my own, I would ask how he wanted me to handle those circumstances. When I left those meetings, I was so confident and charged up that I couldn't wait to accomplish his expectations at a higher level than he expected. That relationship was the foundation of my consulting that evolved into *Partnering with Employees.*

With partnering agreements, mutual expectations cascade through an organization because leaders negotiate expectations with direct reports the same way they negotiate expectations for their own achievement. When leaders and direct reports define and communicate their expectations of each other and negotiate commitments to the expectations, they are engaged in a synergistic transaction that improves the performance of both of them.

Excellent Achievement

Excellent achievement descriptions make expectations specific, measurable, worthwhile, and negotiable. These descriptions should center on quality, quantity, and value.

An excellent level of accomplishment is one that the employee can personally admire and that other people whose respect the employee cherishes will admire. This definition of excellence does not equate with perfection. It equates with projects that are on time and on budget. The level that is mutually agreed to be excellent has to be challenging enough to motivate employees to grow, but not so demanding as to be unrealistic.

Four levels of accomplishment are used. One level is above excellent, because it is important for people to have room for improvement on most expectations. One level below excellent is not desirable, because to most people a good rating means "nothing to be concerned about." It is necessary to be concerned when achievement is below excellent, but people have to be allowed to miss the target without feeling bad about it or they will be reluctant to commit to challenging expectations. What is important is that people know when their achievement of an expectation needs upgrading so that they can focus efforts on improving low achievement rather than feeling bad and wasting energy on negative thoughts. Level one is bad. There is no other way to describe it. No additional levels would serve any useful purpose in this system.

In my surveys of supervisory training participants, I found that most supervisors expect employees to try to be perfect on all assigned tasks all the time. When questioned, these supervisors admitted that perfection is rarely realistic, but both as supervisors and as employees, people believed that aiming for perfection was a helpful expectation. This belief relates to the belief mentioned earlier that employees are at fault for all low achievement. Both beliefs are erroneous.

For example, Roland, the owner of a home mortgage lending company, expected his employees to accomplish a complete exchange of understanding in their communication 100 percent of the time! None of his employees had ever met this expectation. Roland himself had never met it. He said he had read that "people on the average understand about 50 percent of what they hear," and he rated himself at 70 percent. Even though he knew that his expectation was "not realistic," he said, "100 percent is what I want [employees] to think I expect." He also wanted Lauren, his secretary, to think he expected 100 percent error-free letters, when he was actually very happy with her average of about 98 percent and did not want her to spend the additional time it would take to significantly improve on 98 percent accuracy.

Roland expected 100 percent accuracy for loan payment books. He allowed no leeway on that. His company's record was "about one error in 500 on payment books," and here he was willing "to pay the price to get perfection." But, he said, "if we had to pay the price to get perfect performance on everything that every employee does, we'd cost ourselves out of business!"

I pointed out to him that he expected 100 percent but was comfortable with 70 percent communication success; he expected 100 percent correct letters but was comfortable with 98 percent accuracy; and he expected to send accurate payment books to customers 100 percent of the time and nothing less would satisfy him. He agreed that "that's the way it looks," but he was reluctant to tell his employees that 70 percent accuracy for communication, 98 percent for letters, and 100 percent accuracy for payment books were excellent levels of achievement. When I asked him if he thought his leading employees to believe he expected them to be perfect all the time would motivate them to continually improve their performance, he said, "I don't tell them I expect them to be perfect all the time. I just let them know when they make errors."

Roland's attitude contained a serious contradiction. The message that employees typically interpret and respond to when management focuses on errors is, "Mistakes are bad. When I make mistakes, I'm bad. If I make mistakes and get caught, I will probably hear about it and that's bad. I know it is not practical to be perfect at most things, so I will concentrate on not getting caught when I do make mistakes. That keeps employees focused on not getting caught. Roland agreed that this was not the perfection for which he wanted his people to strive.

I asked him, "How does Lauren feel when you do catch a mistake in a letter or in her communication efforts?"

"Devastated. It kills her to make a mistake."

"Even if it was only one out of two hundred letters, or if she communicated successfully 80 percent of the time?"

"Oh sure. Lauren is one in a million. She hates to make mistakes."

"So, . . . even when she might be accomplishing all of her areas of responsibility at a level above what you think is excellent, she would feel devastated about making an error?"

"I've never thought of it that way. But I suppose that's true."

"Wouldn't she have reason to feel good all the time if she knew that 70 percent success for communication and 98 percent accuracy for preparing letters is excellent?"

Our exchange illuminated three points. First, expectations have to be ambitious, achievable, satisfying, and cost effective. Second, achievement expectations have to encourage direct reports to focus on what they want to achieve, to experiment, and to make mistakes and learn from them. Third, people have to accomplish worthwhile commitments to feel self-worth. Roland's expectations and supervisory practices missed all three objectives. He was denying his employees the basis to succeed and to build their self-worth.

Expectations that are not achievable, satisfying, and cost effective are manipulative, a turn-off to employees and a burden to supervisors. For Roland, 70 percent communication success, 98 percent error-free letters, and 100 percent correct payment books were ambitious, achievable, satisfying, and cost-effective criteria that would encourage direct reports to experiment and learn to improve. These criteria defined success.

The training group discussion caused a paradigm shift for Roland. He recognized that his management style was manipulative and it was a relief for him to learn that there was a more satisfying way to influence people.

Excellent Achievement Supports Total Quality Management and Zero Defects

Excellent achievement expectations for less than 100 percent success may appear to contradict the intent of Total Quality Management (TQM) and zero defects programs. In fact, the expectations are an exceptionally efficient means to effect continuous performance improvement and accomplish TQM and zero defects.

Traditional zero defects and TQM performance improvement models view end-product quality as both the stimulus and direction-setter for performance improvement. TQM and zero defects purists presume that everything employees do has an immediate end result product or service. Therefore, purists expect everything employees do to be perfect. However, perfect performance in most expectations is virtually impossible, and most people know this or at least suspect it. To expect 100 percent perfection all of the time is cynical and the essence of win-lose supervision. It causes employees to defend the status quo more often than it influences them to improve their performance.

The philosophy of achieving total customer satisfaction for products and services is laudable and practical. But partnering expectations and achievements are usually not end-result products and services. They are intermediate results that, when taken together, produce end-result customer products and services.

Most excellent achievement expectations are akin to the research and development efforts that go into designing and building a new airplane. The end-product plane has to be perfect for all practical purposes. However, to produce a perfect airplane, millions of procedures, ideas, products, and so forth have to be created, manufactured and tested. And most of these millions of items will fail at first. That is the nature of growth and progress.

Most airplane builders are large bureaucratic organizations. Most bureaucracies are notorious for poor communication with employees. If the average supervisor's communication performance in a bureaucratic organization were evaluated on the criteria in the excellent achievement statements in Exhibit 1.2, the performance would probably rate below 50 percent. Yet the airplanes bureaucratic companies produce are very close to perfect for all practical purposes.

Consider that bureaucratic organizations build virtually perfect planes in win-lose environments with less than 50 percent effective communication. Imagine that plane manufacturing company supervisors expected 70 percent effective communication by employees and helped them achieve it. That would be a 40 percent improvement in communication effectiveness over the 50 percent effectiveness that they achieve by expecting 100 percent effectiveness.

How much less would those virtually perfect planes cost if the manufacturers improved their internal communication accuracy by 40 percent? Employee commitment to and leader support of ambitious and realistic expectations can effect that order of improvement in most areas of responsibility for most employees. Any increased accomplishment in areas of responsibility adds up to lower-cost and higher-quality end-result products and services.

This is not to condone laziness or intentionally poor performance. Ambitious but realistic achievement expectations do not promote the idea that, if excellent achievement is agreed on as 80 percent, then it is okay to mess up the other 20 percent of the time. Instead, excellent achievement criteria eliminate the leverage of mutual ignorance that makes it possible for people to get by with the goof-off practices common in win-lose relationships.

Ambitious but realistic partnering expectations allow for the events and circumstances that are truly beyond employees' ability to control. They promote employee understanding, commitment, and successful, even extraordinarily successful accomplishment. Excellent achievement expectations produce success and recognition of success as a result of employee performance, rather than silence or scorn from supervisors focused on unrealistic goals. Therefore, these expectations promote and support continuous employee performance improvement.

All Achievement Is Quantifiable

Most supervisors believe that many kinds of performance cannot be quantified or measured. I am often asked, how companies can deal with nonperformance issues such as employee compliance with a dress code. My response is that the question is actually about nonproduction expectations rather than nonperformance. Because a dress code is an expectation that usually does not directly affect production, it is difficult to measure in relation to production. However, dress code compliance can be measured simply by counting the times a person does not comply. The consequences of employees' noncompliance with their commitments to a dress code are negotiated into the dress code achievement expectation.

Anything that generates a reaction by an observer can be quantified. Even though many kinds of performance are not customarily measured, they are simple to measure when the right descriptions are used. Excellent achievement statements that are part of negotiated, supported expectations are the right kind of descriptions because they are worded so as to define a basis on which people can quantify degrees of satisfaction or dissatisfaction. Individuals' degrees of dissatisfaction can then form the basis for performance improvement plans that produce satisfaction.

Achievement Expectations Eliminate Employee Grievances

Most work grievances grow out of misunderstandings about the basis for performance evaluation. An example of this was a grievance filed against a division foreman by a maintenance worker in a highway department. The department used five performance rating levels in its performance evaluation system: unacceptable, needs improvement, good, commendable, and outstanding. However, none of the five levels was backed up by an objective, measurable description. In addition, the performance characteristics that foremen were expected to rate did not address unique aspects of different jobs. This situation is true in most organizations whose human resource management systems I have studied. As a result of this kind of rating system, employees find it difficult to connect their ratings to their job achievements. Since supervisors and subordinates in the highway department had not agreed on what observable achievements the five terms described, ratings merely reflected the degree to which supervisors felt their employees were like themselves.

The foreman had rated the maintenance worker an overall good. The worker wanted a commendable rating because it would qualify him for a raise. The grievance hearing was protracted, costly, and vindictive because there was no objective way of comparing actual achievement to the good or commendable ratings. Even after the grievance was arbitrated, departmental work relationships were increasingly adversarial, and no one was satisfied with the results.

Partnering agreements' objective, measurable descriptions of excellent achievement and support commitments eliminate most potential causes of grievances. They make the giving of performance evaluation and feedback a mutually productive and satisfying part of work relationships.

Evaluation and Feedback

Achievement is the outcome of a person's committing to worthwhile goals and then accomplishing them. Achievement evaluation is the way a person learns how well he or she has satisfied his or her own and others' expectations, and decides on cooperative plans to improve performance. Direct reports enjoy reviewing their accomplishments when leaders follow partnering procedures in which evaluations are based on negotiated achievement expectations, and accurately observed accomplishments.

Universal Need for Expectations and Related Feedback

Richard E. Kopelman (1983) summarizes the results of eighteen studies measuring every kind of feedback in diverse sample populations. The tests ran from eight weeks to four years, and in all eighteen of them, objective performance indicators increased after performance review and feedback.

The increases ranged from 6 percent to 125 percent, with a median of 53 percent. The dollar value of savings ranged from $3,500 to $1,000,000, with a median of $91,000. On a per-person basis, the savings ranged from $500 per employee in freight handling to $9,533 per employee in repair shops. The savings realized were more than 100 times greater than the direct costs of accomplishing evaluation and feedback.

From my study of Norman Vincent Peale's books *The Power of Positive Thinking* (1987) and *The Power of Positive Living* (1990), I became much more clear about the profound insight that anything the mind can conceive and believe, people can achieve. In employee partnering, mutual expectations are what the mind can conceive, and continuous evaluation and feedback are what the mind can believe. Any achievement expectation that leaders can define and negotiate, and are willing and able to support, direct reports can and usually do achieve or exceed.

In a master's thesis project on the idea that "employee commitment to excellent achievement and accomplishing it is self actualizing," Richard Platt (1979) worked out an agreement with a construction contractor and a project superintendent to work with two carpentry crews, a test group and a control group. The research location was a large tenant finish project in a shopping mall.

Every morning, the test crew foreman negotiated production budget commitments with his crew and asked the members for ideas to make the work simpler, higher quality, and safer. The foreman always discussed the suggestions with the crew, and when possible, he implemented them. Every evening, he informed the crew of how much they had accomplished compared to what they had committed to in the morning.

The most telling result was the test crew's response to unexpected work demands. On three of the ten test days, the mall owner requested unexpected work to be done immediately. The foreman pulled the test crew off the scheduled work and put them on these unscheduled activities.

The three requests kept the crew off work they had committed to achieve for four hours the first day and two hours on each of two other days. On all three days, the crew finished the extra work and returned and finished more than the amount of the original work to which they had committed. On all ten days, the test crew exceeded the production to which they had committed. Their total production amounted to more than eleven days work in ten days.

The carpenters made it clear that offering ideas about and discussing expectations and being informed of what they actually accomplished were key motivators. They said that these actions made them really want the satisfaction of achieving what they had committed to accomplish.

Most Performance Evaluations Are Nonproductive

Performance evaluation is often fraught with anxiety and mistrust for all parties. As mentioned earlier, W. Edwards Deming (1986, p. 101) rails against traditional performance evaluations as traumatic, deceitful, and debilitating experiences for supervisors and employees alike. Deming's antipathy is justified, for these reasons:

- Most low performance is due to employees' not understanding achievement expectations and not having enough support to accomplish what they assume is expected of them. As a result, most reviews are inadvertently judgmental, coercive, and manipulative, and employees are made to feel guilty for performance results over which they have little control.
- Typical performance standards do not relate to job achievement expectations.
- Lacking a basis of objective achievement measurement criteria, ratings are subjective, often whimsical, rarely mutually agreeable, and seldom support performance improvement.
- When expectations are specific and measurable, they usually relate to bottom-

line-oriented production objectives; they rarely show employees what behavior to improve.
- Performance ratings rank employees against each other, so only the top-ranked person can feel successful.
- Performance improvement plans rarely address supervisory shortcomings that cause low achievement.
- Most supervisory effort is spent on the low performers, who cause problems; the best performers are usually ignored and denied the assistance that could help them be even better.

Ranking Employees Is Destructive

Ordinary performance review ratings are commonly used to rank employees for the purposes of determining compensation distribution. Ranking performance ratings causes employees to question their self-worth and to focus their attention and energies on outranking their peers rather than on cooperating with them. All too often outranking peers means being destructive to them. This activity is inherently damaging to individuals and to organizations. (A more effective means of allocating compensation is discussed in Chapter Seven.)

The concept of ranking individuals is a philosophy of scarcity. One person's gain can come only at another's loss. When employees are ranked, only one can totally succeed. Furthermore, because the most common causes of a low ranking are supervisory shortcomings beyond employees' ability to control, ordinary reviews are more likely to tear down supervisor-employee relationships than to build them up.

The concept of team achievement reviews is a philosophy of plenty. When people are rated on achievement compared to their personal commitments, everyone has the opportunity to be totally successful. Every person can successfully meet excellent achievement expectations.

The employees of one defense contractor call the forced ranking at the end of performance reviews the "Tomahawk" because that is where all employees get chopped up. The professionals in this company are very bright and used to being at the top of the grading system in school and college. Their achievement is a primary reason for their being hired. However, in the forced ranking, some of the professionals are at the bottom no matter how well they performed. Even when there is only a fraction of a percentage point separating top- and bottom-ranked employees, being ranked low is devastating for people accustomed to being at the top. Moreover, these rankings do not acknowledge supervisory shortcomings or help people discover how to do better.

Recently, I was invited to be part of two training sessions conducted for sixty supervisors of a large public utility, and I saw a situation that illustrated all seven of my reasons why performance reviews are typically counterproductive. My invitation was a result of the executive team members' having read a prepublication manuscript of this book.

The utility is operating under the cloud of a large number of job reductions in the parent company's other branches. The utility's employees were told that no cuts were expected in their company for the upcoming fiscal year. They also were told that the utility was expected to increase its production by 25 percent over the previous year's objectives, with no personnel increase.

An executive planning committee arbitrarily concluded that 25 percent of company employees were performing below the previous year's production objectives. The original plan was to rate all employees' performances and designate 25 percent of them as "at risk of termination." The performance of the at risk employees was to be brought up to current production expectations and then increased 25 percent beyond that to meet the new standard set for all employees. Notwithstanding the statement that no job cuts were planned, a representative group of employees asked to examine the plan because they interpreted the planning team's goal as a ranking process to find and terminate 25 percent of them. To them, the "at risk of termination" language overshadowed the real goal of increasing production. The planning committee dropped the quota, but kept the rest of the goal.

In unilateral actions, supervisors were to rate their own perceptions of all of their employees' performances against the previous year's production objectives. The first training session was designed to show all the company supervisors how to do this rating.

Then the supervisors were to meet with employees who were not at risk to tell them their performance was all right. Supervisors were also to prepare remedial performance improvement plans for at risk employees, and submit the plans to higher-level supervisors and company human relations staff for approval.

Once the remedial plans were approved, supervisors were to meet one-on-one with their at risk employees and inform them that they had been evaluated, determined to be at risk, and would be required to implement the approved plan. These employees were to be invited to discuss whatever they wanted to discuss, but by company policy, supervisors were required to enforce the plans as approved. They could discuss but not negotiate. Employees were also to be invited to sign the plans. If anyone refused, supervisors were instructed to record on the plans the employee's refusal. The second training session taught supervisors how to break the at risk news and explain the rating conclusions and improvement plans.

Over the weeks that this activity was going on, the planning committee realized that they were not satisfied with the long-term implications of their performance management process. Feedback from the employee review group and the executive team's review of my manuscript caused the team to realize that the process was win-lose employee manipulation. Although the planning committee is following through with the procedures as described, they are considering partnering with employees as a new direction for this year.

Evaluation Should Focus on Achievement

One primary value of feedback is that it produces an accurate understanding of achievement deficiencies. These deficiencies then become employees' targets for improvement. Useful information on deficiencies comes from evaluating achievement, not performance. "Performance" in most companies is action, not results, and only results have measurable value. Because it has been defined in the partnering agreement, "achievement" is worthwhile and measurable. Therefore, achievement is the evaluation focus in employee partnering.

Lawrence Miller (1984, p. 99) offers an example of the high value of relevant and factual feedback to achievement results. An hourly worker in a textile mill, whose job had precisely engineered achievement standards, consistently accomplished only 35 percent of those standards. Managers tolerated Mary because she had perfect attendance while the other employees' attendance was poor. However, when overall attendance improved, Mary's manager began to view her achievement as unacceptable. He graphed her performance, showed it to her, and asked if she thought she could improve. When she said yes, he asked her if a goal of 45 percent would be a comfortable target, and she agreed to that goal. The manager plotted Mary's achievement on the graph daily, and they both discussed it.

Each time Mary accomplished a goal, they repeated the process, and Mary offered a new goal. No one made a negative remark or coercive request during the discussions. The positive focus on Mary and her performance and the positive recognition of her progressive achievement caused her to reach a level of 120 percent of standard and to stay there. The power released when she committed to expectations and received accurate feedback produced a nearly fourfold improvement in her achievement.

Ratings Reflect Perceptions of Achievement

Perceptions strongly influence relationships. Ideal work relationships are those in which leaders and direct reports perceive that their interactions are productive and mutually satisfying. Perceptions of situations commonly differ from the facts of situations, but perceptions are as much a reality as facts. Therefore, partnering evaluations must deal with perceptions.

Partnering does not use rating numbers to describe or rank people. Partnering ratings are objective conclusions drawn from *both* leaders' and direct reports' subjective perceptions about direct reports' accomplishments. The process of rating is intended to stimulate and support true dialogue on comparing perceptions of achievement. Honestly perceived low ratings, regardless of objective accuracy, reflect relationship stress points. Stress points are indicators of opportunities to improve relationships, leadership support, and team achievement.

The experience of a client of mine illustrates how the ratings work. For eighteen months, Ashley, an estimator, and Jack, a company owner, had difficult and sometimes angry exchanges about one report that Ashley provides to Jack.

Then they began using a partnering agreement that included the expectation that Ashley would prepare reports. Jack respected Ashley as an exceptionally effective estimator; however, he rated her a 2 on the report preparation expectation while Ashley rated herself a 3.2.

Ashley always went the extra mile to make sure her reports had the most accurate and up-to-date information. When they compared their perceptions, Jack agreed that she always had accurate and up-to-date reports, but he also said to her, "I've been trying to tell you every month with my memos and harangues, [that] it's critical that I get the information from you on the fourth of each month. I have to prepare a report for the bank that they want by the seventh. . . . I cannot get it to them on time if I don't get your report on the fourth. . . . Having your data on the fourth is critical to me. It affects how I am able to run this company."

As Ashley and Jack discussed this situation, it turned out that this was the only reason Jack rated Ashley low.

Ashley said, "Here all along I have been thinking about that report the way I think about estimating. My estimating success depends on my using the latest and best possible information. My habit of always waiting for the latest information has kept me from really hearing what you've been asking for all this time. When I know some big items are coming in soon after the fourth, I've waited to include them in the report, thinking that the important business would help you. . . . Now that I understand what you need, it will be easier than what I've been doing."

Ashley then made a critical point about the value of partnering's feedback process when she said, "I wonder how long it would have taken us to get through to each other if we hadn't compared our perceptions of my performance of this expectation?"

Honest Ratings Are Accurate Ratings

In partnering, all honest ratings are accurate ratings. Whether or not a perception of achievement is objectively factual, perception is what people live and operate by. A perception is an honest description of feeling. An honest description of feeling is a variety of fact. Ratings are not in error when they reflect honest perceptions of achievement.

Another example illustrates how a ratings discussion can help people deal with perceptions that result when personal issues intrude into work relationships. Annette is a single female administrative assistant. Her leader, Fazel, is a single male. During their first review based on a partnering agreement, he rated her communication achievement 1.9 while she rated it 3. I was observing, and it was evident that they were uncomfortable talking about this expectation. Fazel asked, "Annette, what were you thinking when you rated your communication performance?"

Annette sidestepped the question, "What were you thinking when you rated me?"

"I'm hoping it will help me put my thoughts into words if you go first. Would you help me by doing that?"

"I know what I think. I can't understand why you have such a different rating."

"Well, . . . maybe we can clear it up if you start."

Finally, Annette said she had made a conscious effort to make sure her messages were always taken accurately and passed on the same way. She had even practiced and felt that she had improved in asking people to reflect back what they understood from her instructions. She made a conscious effort to be friendly, so people would like communicating with her.

Fazel nodded agreement several times as she was talking. When she mentioned being friendly, he grimaced, and Annette asked what was wrong.

"You just touched on the reason I rated you low."

"You rated me down for trying to be friendly to people?"

"No, I rated you down because I can't understand you."

"Now I do not understand you. What don't you understand about me?"

"I think you communicate in your job really well. I like it that you are really friendly. You seem very friendly to me too, except when I've invited you to spend social time with me. Every time I've done that, you've said no and then acted cold to me for several days. I do not understand why."

"If that is why you rated me low, I do not understand what that has to do with how well I communicate in my job."

"Do you dislike me?"

"Heavens, no. I like you a lot."

"It seems to me that makes my point. I have assumed that you like me, but when I try to show that I like you too, I get the cold shoulder. I know I am trying to communicate with you, but I do not feel like you are communicating with me."

"But why do you rate me down for something that has nothing to do with how I do my job?"

"Because it affects how I do my job. It affects how I relate to you. How I relate to you affects how you relate to others. You may think that my feelings are not your fault and you would be right. But the fact is, I do have feelings about you."

"But why rate me down? I do not see how it's my fault that you have a problem understanding why I'm not comfortable going out with you."

"I didn't rate you low to blame you. I even agree that it's my problem. I rated you low because I thought doing so would precipitate an exchange that would improve our work relationship. Isn't that the main reason we're doing this?"

Annette then said that her reaction to Fazel was not personal. She said, "I had a very bitter experience in a previous job where I was taken advantage of by my boss. I did not consciously contribute to that problem but I sure have suffered for it. I vowed that I would never allow that to happen again. I'm sorry for reacting so coldly to you when you asked me out. But I just can't even think of dating my boss, no matter how much I may like you as a leader."

Personal feelings do become entangled in work relationships and often adversely affect people's work. Partnering agreement evaluations offer a setting in which people can discuss their perceptions candidly and safely, relating them to work issues and not to personalities. This kind of discussion often results in leaders and reports designing an expectation for their partnering agreement to remedy specific problems. In this instance, the remedy did not require a written plan—Fazel agreed to stop asking Annette for a date.

Partnering Procedures Assure Accurate Ratings

Leaders' and direct reports' primary objective in partnering achievement reviews is to agree to focus on one or two expectations for improvement. The review procedures plus this objective discourage lazy efforts and intentionally dishonest ratings. When ratings are mostly the same, it is difficult to decide where relationship stress points are. Rating expectations accurately simplifies deciding which expectations are the most important ones to improve. In contrast, traditional performance evaluations require supervisors to do more paperwork to justify any rating that is above or below average; thus, honest, above- or below-average ratings are discouraged.

For example, a director of human resources for a school district notes that it is rare for school principals to rate teachers above or below average. It takes about four hours to accomplish a rating if there is nothing out of the ordinary, but about two days to complete all the extra paperwork and discussions with higher officials when a high or a low rating is given. The director says that, under these conditions, "All the ratings do is satisfy statutory requirements; they are a complete waste of time and money" for the people who should benefit from them.

A widely held belief about human performance is that behavior is a function of its consequences. Rewarded behavior increases and ignored behavior diminishes. I share this belief because I have witnessed these behavioral changes. Just one example was what happened during a meeting with the president of a sheetmetal and roofing company, his four direct reports, and the five people who reported to the president's reports. All nine reports had negotiated partnering agreements four months earlier, agreements which included Leadership Support Agreements with the statement, "I expect and will welcome feedback on my leadership performance."

Earlier in the week, Randy, the president, had rated his four direct reports—one of whom was his cousin Ed. All the reports had also rated their own achievements on the 1 to 4 scale described earlier. They had exchanged their rating numbers two days before the evaluation meeting, and each report had a table with his or her own ratings side by side with Randy's ratings (see Table 1.2).

Randy modeled the evaluation procedures by dialoguing about achievement perceptions, one person at a time, with his four direct reports. Ed was the third person whom Randy addressed. He asked Ed which expectation Ed wanted to discuss first, and Ed said project management.

Randy wasn't sure what to expect of the discussion because Ed was a soft-spoken person who would go to extremes to avoid confrontation. Randy had rated Ed a 1.5 on this expectation, while Ed had rated himself a 3.5. Randy asked what Ed was thinking of when he rated himself.

Ed replied, "Every one of my projects during the period came in on or ahead of schedule and on or under budget."

There was a considerable pause, and Randy looked a little tense. Ed was ashen. The rest of us sat motionless.

Randy finally said, "My rating reflects the result of your work on the Federal Heights project. We lost 22 percent on that one."

Ed replied, "I know that, Randy, but remember in March when you got real interested and started taking calls from the owner? We were having mixed signals, so I backed off, and you took it over completely. When I was running it, it was on time and under budget. It was after you took it over that it went to pot. I knew what was happening, but I didn't want to interfere."

There was a long silence. Thoughtfully, Randy replied, "You're right. When I think back on it, that's exactly what happened. On second thought, I have no reason to rate you less than a 3.5 on that expectation." After another considerable pause, Randy said that he would change his rating to a 3.5. He also said he was surprised and pleased that Ed stood his ground, and asked Ed why he had spoken up. Ed described Randy's leadership support commitment statement about welcoming constructive feedback. Ed said, "Since you signed that statement, I trusted that you meant it."

After that, Ed and Randy talked at some length as though there was no one else in the room. They agreed upon ways to communicate more easily and effectively in the future. They decided that any time Ed had feedback for Randy, Ed would ask Randy, "When would be a good time for a discussion on some feedback?" It was agreed that the answer would always be a specific time and place, or at least a date when a time and place would be decided.

That kind of dialogue fit Randy's style, so the whole conversation was easy and satisfying for him. It was far from easy, but it was even more satisfying for Ed. Randy has since discovered some valuable capabilities in Ed that he had never seen before. That experience was the beginning of a more productive and satisfying relationship, which rested on the commitment Randy made to welcome (reward) constructive feedback.

Employees Initiate Agreements and Evaluations

Negotiated expectations and performance evaluation and feedback form the ideal mechanism through which direct reports can help their leaders improve their leadership performance. Reports can even take the initiative for negotiating an agreement and reviewing their achievement with their leaders, as in the case that follows.

Dale, the owner of an electrical contracting company, was a hard-nosed self-made autocrat who kept his employees dependent on him. His nephew, Ron, was vice president of the company, under an agreement that he would take over when Dale retired.

Ron and Dale's work relationship was contentious for several reasons. The most distressing, to Ron, was Dale's constant complaining about Ron's preparation of contract estimates. Dale would not allow a bid to be submitted without his review and approval; however, he also refused to review Ron's estimates or respond to questions about them before they were complete. Every time Ron submitted finished estimates, Dale demanded major changes. Ron became sick of treatment that crushed his confidence and self-esteem. After a year of employment, Ron convinced Dale to work out an achievement agreement between them, even though Dale refused to offer any support commitments. At that point, Ron was content to clarify Dale's expectations. Six months after the agreement was in place, they started an achievement review. Ron had rated himself a 4 on the expectation that he would prepare estimates, while Dale had rated Ron a 1. When Ron asked what Dale was thinking when he rated Ron a 1, Dale pointed out they nearly always had to change Ron's estimates. Ron agreed that that was true. Then he asked if Dale was still committed to Ron's learning estimating so he could be responsible for it when Dale retired. When Dale said he was, Ron asked if Dale could recall any estimate that Ron had submitted in the last six months in which Dale found fault with any take-offs, expansions, or labor estimates. When Dale agreed that he hadn't found fault with those areas, Ron explained, "I rated myself on the part of estimating that is in my sphere of control—take-offs, expansions, and labor estimates. As you just agreed, you haven't had a single occasion to question that part of my estimates. The items you've asked me to change are discretionary, like how we distribute overhead or how we want to define profits. I always go to great pains to address the discretionary items the way you accepted them on previous similar projects. But you refuse to discuss anything about my estimates before I submit them to you. When I do submit them, you have used different criteria to evaluate them every time. Therefore it's not possible for me to know what you want."

"Are you saying that your performance rating is right and mine is wrong?" Dale demanded.

Ron answered, "I'm only explaining why I rated myself a 4. By your own admission, I have done nearly a perfect job on estimating issues that are possible to learn. You wait to see what I've decided and then you choose something else. There is no way for me to win on that score."

"Well, that's the way it is Ron," said Dale, "I own the business and you're the hired help."

"Uncle Dale, are you worried about my taking over too much before you are ready to let go?"

". . . Is that what you think, . . . that I rated you low just to keep you in your place?"

"The only thing I am sure of is that my rating is accurate for the achievement that we agreed to in this expectation. I desperately want to gain your confidence in me as an estimator and as a total electrical contractor. I want you to be sure of me when you're ready for me to take over. If that's what you want, then I need help from you that I have not had up to now."

Dale asked what kind of help Ron would suggest, and Ron asked for two things. He wanted to know specifically what Dale wanted him to achieve, and he wanted Dale to stick to those expectations. He also wanted Dale to make it possible for Ron to achieve Dale's expectations.

Dale then suggested that Ron start writing policies for the estimating decisions he had been making. Dale would tell Ron how to perfect the policies, and then Dale would allow Ron to go by those policies instead of having to get Dale's approval. Ron asked if they could do that with all policy-related matters in addition to the estimating issues, and Dale agreed that would be a "good way" for them to get their "heads together for the transition."

Ron assumed the leadership role in this partnering procedure because Dale refused to do so. Ron was not controlling Dale, but Ron was in control of the discussion. Even though the agreement was initially devoid of support commitments, the agreement empowered Ron to take the initiative to achieve his goal. Ron's persistence effected a change in Dale's attitude, so that he agreed to support Ron through newly developed company policies. That agreement greatly enhanced the chances for a successful transfer of company leadership at a later time. Eventually, Ron was able to work out an agreement that included support commitments.

The principles discussed in Chapters Three and Four are built into the partnering leadership procedures described in Part Two of this book. When leaders follow the procedures, they follow the principles. In following the principles, they create and support synergistic work relationships that result in individuals' rewarding each other for efforts to achieve specific expectations. Synergistic relationships make win-win cultures a reality.

4

Making It Work: Addressing Challenges to Implementation

Implementing employee partnering challenges both management and employees. For management, the challenge is to model employee partnering procedures. In win-lose cultures, top management all too often expects subordinate managers and supervisors to change to improve organizational performance, but modeling good leadership procedures cannot be delegated. The procedures have to be implemented and sustained at all levels, starting at the top.

The primary challenge for employees is to learn that partnering is not yet another way for supervisors to manipulate employees to produce more and better. Even under the best of organizational conditions, employees may initially mistrust management efforts to change organizational cultures. Modeling the procedures is the key to overcoming the mistrust.

Leaders Must Model What They Expect

Implementation of employee partnering agreements must start with the top leader in an organization or a subdivision. However, not all organizational levels must be implemented simultaneously. For example, if an organization has six levels of management, partnering could be implemented in all six levels in one combined effort, in the top three levels first and three remaining management levels later, or in two levels at a time. No supervisory or management levels should be skipped. Partnering will not work well at levels one and two if it is implemented in levels six, five, and four, but not in level three.

Partnering necessitates major improvements in leadership behavior. People instinctively resist being pushed into change, yet employees easily follow what their leaders model, whether that modeling is for or against change. When supervisors resist change themselves, employees understand that it is all right to defend the status quo. If supervisors at level three do not model the partnering procedures, supervisors in levels two and one have no immediate model to follow and do not receive the message that they must change. The following case study illustrates the practical reasons why leaders should model what they expect.

Case Study: Master Metals of La Crosse, Wisconsin

The experience of Master Metals of La Crosse, Wisconsin, in introducing partnering exemplifies how an organization must deal with employee mistrust of management caused by previous win-lose experiences. By using partnering agreements, however, company president Richard Bott was able to lead his team quickly to a win-win organizational culture.

Richard began by distributing partnering agreement drafts to his employees. As he distributed the drafts, he explained a little about partnering procedures and his reasons for implementing them. Then he scheduled a meeting for two weeks later with Brenda, the office manager, Jeff, the shop manager, and Rich, the field general superintendent. He also scheduled a second meeting with the field foremen.

Initial Mistrust of Management

On Monday of the meeting week, Richard asked the field foremen individually what they thought of the agreements and accompanying procedures. Their responses all supported his desire to implement partnering with employees. However, on the day before the first negotiating meeting, Rich, the general superintendent talked to each of the field foremen and heard an opposite response. Rich made a list of field foremen concerns and read them to Richard over the phone.

The concerns worried Richard, and when I arrived to facilitate the meetings, Richard explained that he had emphasized performance evaluations in his initial discussions with his supervisors. Because he was not yet familiar with partnering evaluations, he had described a traditional evaluation process. I concluded that the supervisors' contradictory responses probably reflected their feelings about traditional performance reviews.

When we started the first meeting, Rich wanted to address his list of concerns immediately. I suggested that, ideally, we should address those issues as soon as we reached a consensus on a meeting objective. Following is the objective Richard, Rich, Brenda, and Jeff developed:

> We want to establish and sustain working relationships that result in:
>
> 1. An abundance of satisfied and repeat customers
> 2. Employees feeling fulfillment and prospering according to their capability and their efforts
> 3. A profitable company for which employees can work as long as they want to and are productive

After everyone voiced individual enthusiasm for the objective, Rich read the following list of the foremen's concerns:

1. They lack understanding of the agreement draft that they received so they are very skeptical about this whole program.
2. They do not believe that a proper line of communication can be established at this date. Possibly an intermediary person would help.
3. They have heard the story for years of all contractors' losing money on almost every job. They want to know how the program will bring integrity to relations with management and how it will benefit them.
4. For [the facilitator] to get accurate feedback from the field foremen on their feelings about this program, Richard Bott must not be present, which will assure field foremen of confidentiality.
5. Who keeps the records of our performance ratings?
6. Who determines each field foreman's performance shortfalls and the reasons for the performance ratings?
7. What use will be made of our performance ratings?
8. There is the traditional feeling that written records are kept only for employers' benefit to be used against employees when the need arises.
9. They want assurance that the shortcomings identified in their performance reviews *will not* result in any pay loss. Good jobs are available elsewhere.
10. On the subject of checks and balances:

    - Who determines the expectations for the Boss [Richard Bott]?
    - [Expectations] should be determined only after talking to all the employees. This would help to open up communications.
    - Who determines performance ratings for the Boss?

11. To date this company has tried four different supervisory and foremen programs and all of them have died from lack of interest and support from the office.
12. About the suggested idea that this will help employees' self advancement: company paid registration fees have been available to employees for local technical college classes for six years. But there has been minimal employee participation.
13. We believe we have the best crew that has been assembled in the last 25 years. It only needs to be cultivated.
14. You [the boss and the facilitator] will have to sell me and the

> others on the fact that all parties will try and open good communication lines or the program will fail. Lots of luck.

As Rich read his concerns, Richard Bott looked puzzled while Brenda's and Jeff's body language showed that they supported Rich's comments. When Rich finished, I asked, "Do you believe these concerns are unique to this company?"

Rich said, "Probably not. . . . We've all worked for other companies. These problems are not as bad here as they were in other companies. . . . But they are problems here."

This is the procedure I used to address his concerns. I said, "I'd like you to know how profound and valuable those comments are. I've heard them thousands of times in supervisory training programs that I've taught. I have also heard them from peers and experienced them as an employee. The fact that so many people feel this way makes your comments all the more important. They describe the very kinds of concerns that led to the development of employee partnering agreements. They point out the dominating win-lose work relationships that are a serious problem in most organizations, not just Master Metals."

Then I asked Rich a question, "Relationships must be much better than average here or you wouldn't be making these comments, would you?" Rich agreed that things were better at Master Metals than in most other companies.

So I asked him, "Do you believe the Master Metals' team can achieve the objective that all of you agreed to earlier?"

"You do not have a problem getting me to cooperate," Rich answered. "I'm just telling you what you are up against."

From Mistrust to Mutual Trust

After that dialogue, we were able to discuss all the items to everyone's satisfaction. Richard Bott made comments and answered questions from his point of view. I supported his comments and supplied additional information. Rich, Brenda, and Jeff liked what they understood of partnering and negotiated several achievement expectations with Richard.

The next morning, the second meeting got underway. After a brief discussion, the field foremen eagerly supported the previously negotiated meeting objective. However, they made it clear that they did not trust ordinary performance reviews. Jeff explained how achievement evaluations are conducted in partnering relationships. After that, it took less than five minutes of discussion for the foremen to understand and express satisfaction with Jeff's explanation.

Rich again read his list of concerns, and the foremen agreed that the statements accurately represented their feelings. Everyone participated freely. Then, in the middle of the discussion on their concern that management keeps evaluation records to use against employees, Richard Bott blurted out, "Just a minute, I have something to say. I have not said much up to now because I want you to feel free to say what you want to say. But I have to tell you that some of what I have been hearing about my leadership is not very flattering. I'll be honest with you, it doesn't feel very good to hear it. I have worked hard for many years not to do what you've been saying you do not like about management." Then he had a revelation. He said, "I just realized that you haven't been talking directly about Richard Bott, owner of Master Metals. You're venting a life time of mistrust and frustration with John Doe Manager of any company! . . . Is that the message you're sending?"

The foremen confirmed that Richard was on target. One of the foremen said, "This is the best work team I have ever been a part of. But I assumed we were addressing ways to make communication and other working conditions even better. That's why I haven't said anything up to now about how good we have it in this company."

Another foreman pointed out that the program called for them to "change a lifetime of attitudes and habits." He said, "We have a lot of mistrust about being manipulated by management to get out of our systems before we're comfortable with operating this way. But don't take that to mean we do not want to make the improvements. We know we're in an unusually good situation, or we wouldn't even have this opportunity." That dialogue led into negotiating Achievement Expectations that were to turn out especially well.

Six months after these negotiations, Richard reported that the company had been in a very difficult position when the agreements were implemented. The market was tough and competition was brutal. Eight months later, the team had pulled together and the company was nine times more profitable than nine months earlier. Richard felt that the only thing to which he could attribute the change was that he implemented the agreements. He said, "Following the agreements, my team did the rest to improve our productivity, increase our ability to win more bids, and help us make more profit."

Partnering Paperwork

Paperwork is disliked by supervisors and employees alike, and most individuals' first impression is that partnering procedures may require excessive paperwork. However, in this case, first impressions should be reconsidered. The questions to be answered are, What is paperwork? and, Excessive compared to what?

Paperwork is perceived as burdensome because it is all too often repetitive documentation. Partnering agreements are not repetitive documentation. They are new information, the result of thoughtful consideration of ideas, feelings, challenges, expectations, and commitments. They redefine bases on which team members can communicate completely with each other. In addition, they directly produce trust, cooperation, and improved performance. Agreements are documented, but their application, purpose, and results are far different from the routine of typical paperwork. Leaders and direct reports continually revise existing expectations and sometimes add new ones. Once the initial papers are prepared, ongoing paperwork is perceived in terms of the value to be gained from the communication efforts incorporated in the partnering process.

If organizations have no typed job expectations, partnering agreements will use decidedly more paper. Agreements also usually have more pages than simple job descriptions. However, job descriptions are rarely productive. Partnering agreements are productive and can actually reduce the overall paperwork required to administer employee relations in large organizations.

A person who works for an old-line railroad company and who reviewed the manuscript for this book said, "If our company were to use partnering agreements, it would allow us to get rid of performance development reviews, job descriptions, management by objective forms, performance development plans, management behavior questionnaires, and career planning forms. There may be even more [we could do without]." Thus, for organizations with detailed administrative procedures, partnering agreements result in far less paperwork, because one agreement can fulfill the purposes of all the items the reviewer mentioned.

The most important difference between repetitive paperwork and partnering agreements is that the agreements improve working relationships. What is the value of productive and mutually satisfying work relationships in terms of the number of pages it takes to accomplish these relationships? Most true leaders will say, "However many pages it takes!"

Partnering Supports Deming's Fourteen Quality Points

W. Edwards Deming created a list of fourteen points about management (originally published in Deming, 1986, and updated by Deming in 1990) that describe the basics of his philosophy.

1. Create and publish to all employees a statement of the aims and purposes of the company or other organization. The management must demonstrate constantly their commitment to this statement.
2. Learn the new philosophy, top management and everybody.
3. Understand the purpose of inspection, for improvement of processes and reduction of cost.
4. End the practice of awarding business on the basis of price tag alone.
5. Improve constantly and forever the system of production and service.
6. Institute training.
7. Teach and institute leadership.
8. Drive out fear. Create trust. Create a climate for innovation.
9. Optimize toward the aims and purposes of the company the efforts of teams, groups, staff areas.
10. Eliminate exhortations for the work force.

11.a. Eliminate numerical quotas for production. Instead, learn and institute methods for improvement.
   b. Eliminate M.B.O. [Management by Objectives]. Instead, learn the capabilities of processes, and how to improve them.
12. Remove barriers that rob people of pride of workmanship.
13. Encourage education and self-improvement for everyone.
14. Take action to accomplish the transformation.

Implementing employee partnering directly supports all of Deming's points.

Point one. Partnering agreements result in the leader–direct-report team improvement efforts that will contribute the most to the employer's mission, and thus encourage constancy of purpose.

Point two. Employee partnering is a tangible and structured win-win model of the new philosophy to which Deming alludes. Partnering addresses quality in terms of work relationships, and it addresses achievement by defining, negotiating, supporting, and achieving excellence for every area of responsibility included in a partnering agreement.

Point three. Because individuals negotiate the quality terms for which they are personally accountable, they are empowered to accomplish their quality commitments.

Point four. Partnering procedures model the kinds of considerations, mutual trust, and win-win transactions that are necessary to end the practice of awarding business on price tag alone, because competition between vendors is not necessary to keep their prices in line.

Point five. Every achievement review results in performance improvement plans, assuring that constant improvement is a part of every employee's conscious thoughts, commitments, and actions. In addition, partnering procedures model a method, as required by Deming, for accomplishing this improvement.

Point six. Employee partnering requires targeted training and retraining when low achievement is caused by the lack of knowledge or skill.

Point seven. Employee partnering transforms supervisors from enforcers to true leaders who support employees' achievement. Instituting employee partnering institutes leadership.

Point eight. Leadership support commitments, negotiated achievement expectations, and the specific support for each expectation all act directly and effectively to empower employees and drive out employee fear.

Point nine. Barriers between staff areas result from win-lose turf battles. The win-win cultures produced by employee partnering eliminate most of the circumstances that create these barriers.

Point ten. Slogans and exhortations are irrelevant in employee partnering. Negotiated commitments for leadership support and employee achievement are the influences that produce the greatest accomplishment.

Point eleven. Numerical quotas cause people to focus on only one measure of worth, the quantity of products or services finished in a given period. Negotiated expectations systematically assure that all important aspects of products, services, and customer interests are appropriately considered by all employees all of the time.

Point twelve. Meeting excellent levels of achievement produces feelings of self-worth and pride of workmanship.

Point thirteen. Although a program of education and retraining is not built into partnering, the review process establishes desired achievement levels, measures actual achievement, identifies specific deficiencies, and targets appropriate remedies, thereby producing the information needed to establish and sustain a company education and training program that will meet acknowledged needs.

Point fourteen. Implementing employee partnering agreements accomplishes a Total Quality Management transformation. Partnering does not replace steps in the Total Quality Management implementation process. Instead, it is the often missing part that will minimize the organizational pain, strain, and financial drain of influencing employees to understand and commit to total quality achievement.

Deming also identifies "Seven Deadly Diseases" of management (1986):

1. Lack of constancy of purpose
2. Emphasis on short-term profits
3. Evaluation by performance, merit rating, or annual review
4. Mobility of top management
5. Running a company on visible figures alone ("counting the money")
6. Excessive medical costs
7. Excessive costs of warranty, fueled by lawyers that work on contingency fee

Employee partnering helps management avoid or "cure" these common diseases.

Disease one. Partnering's response to this serious problem is also its answer to Deming's point one. Partnering agreements set out an organization's vision, mission, and its constancy of purpose in a way that relates these goals to each employee's job.

Disease two. Employee partnering emphasizes continuous and long-term improvement and customer satisfaction. Partnering is based on the premise that the long-term view produces the best overall profits.

Disease three. Partnering eliminates ordinary performance reviews that hold employees to blame for most of their low achievement.

Disease four. Partnering makes continued employment in the same organization much more attractive and beneficial to individual employees. They know how they can grow within their present organization and can contrast that to the uncertainties of frequent job hopping.

Disease five. The partnering philosophy recognizes that visible figures are the final test of organizational stability but that these figures say nothing about how to effect individual improvement. Employee partnering allows managers to run companies by creating many specific areas of individual responsibility and improvement.

Disease six. Partnering reduces stress and reduces the time needed to accomplish production, thus reducing stress-related medical costs.

Disease seven. Higher quality of achievement and customer satisfaction resulting from partnering reduces the need for and cost of legal services.

These analyses demonstrate that employee partnering and the leadership procedures that make it work are the infrastructure for Total Quality Management.

Part Two

PARTNERING IN ACTION

5

Preparing and Negotiating Partnering Agreements

The leadership expectations in partnering agreements call for supervisors to accomplish exceptionally progressive and effective human relations transactions. Supervisors can succeed at these transactions and be transformed into leaders even if they have not received specific human relations training. They succeed when the following simple conditions are present:

- As leaders in organizations, supervisors accept accomplishing the procedures as a condition of employment.
- The negotiated and signed leadership support commitments empower direct reports and leaders to negotiate candidly and assertively with each other.
- During implementation, each partnering procedure is demonstrated by an internal or external facilitator and practiced by each leader as it applies to the needs of the moment.
- The potentially most difficult to talk about human relations issues are addressed and resolved during facilitated implementation exchanges.
- All organization leaders except the one at the top negotiate their own partnering agreements as the direct reports of their own leaders before they negotiate as leaders with their own direct reports.
- Leaders and direct reports experience success and satisfaction in dealing with ordinary and difficult issues during facilitated implementation sessions.

Customizing Expectations

The objective in customizing expectations is to influence leaders and direct reports to understand and own the support and achievement expectations in the agreement drafts for specific jobs.

At the start of partnering implementation, all employees are given drafts of agreements for their jobs. Leaders also review drafts for their direct reports' jobs. Both leaders and direct reports are expected to individually customize the draft contents to their own satisfaction prior to their getting together to negotiate.

Leaders and direct reports first address the leadership support expectations, because the consideration of support responsibilities is what gets supervisors to begin thinking and acting as true leaders. After customizing the support page, leaders customize all the other expectations in their agreement drafts. In addition to changing the wording in the achievement expectations as necessary, both leaders and direct reports decide the preliminary percentages that they will use to define excellent achievement for each excellent achievement statement.

This initial customizing activity has proven exceptionally informative and satisfying for all levels of managers. A case in point is the president of a national wholesale distributing firm who has been in his position for over ten years and who manages thirteen regional sales divisions. His direct reports are a controller, marketing director, operations director, human resources director, and the thirteen regional managers. The job of managing the whole operation was literally stressing him to ill health.

At a strategic planning retreat, the direct reports made it painfully clear to the president that they were frustrated and not sure what he expected of them. They also had no idea what support they could expect from him or the other four home-office professionals. Up to that time, the director hadn't known what his reports were doing or thinking. Therefore, when he received the partnering agreement drafts, he marvelled at how they clarified his understanding of job responsibilities. For the first time, he felt he knew what he wanted to accomplish and what he wanted each of his people to accomplish. It was the beginning of a satisfying way to lead without controlling, which he was loath to do. He also experienced less stress. He now keeps his copy of his direct reports' agreements near his elbow, so he can refer to them easily and regularly. His direct reports have had similar experiences using their agreements.

Negotiating Agreements

The objective of negotiating agreements is to produce win-win agreements that leaders and direct reports can comfortably sign.

To achieve this comfort, leaders and direct reports must be empowered by being in control of what they commit to accomplish. Being empowered in relationships with supervisors is a radical change for most employees, and they must be convinced that their leaders sincerely want them to be in control of what they commit to. Leaders convince employees of this when the leaders start the partnering meeting by negotiating and signing the leadership support commitments. (See Exhibit 1.1. on p. 14)

The act of negotiating support commitments models ideal communication and leadership. The typical results of this modeling are demonstrated in this example of partnering within a government agency. I was facilitating a negotiating session with Jake, a supervisor, and his direct report Cameron. Jake asked Cameron, "How do feel about negotiating to clarify my support for you?"

Cameron said he did not know, because he had "never heard of subordinates being invited to question their bosses' commitment for support."

Jake said, "Then let me be more specific. How would it work best for you to ask for more support when you feel that you need it?"

Cameron still said it was "difficult" to respond to that question.

Jake asked, "Is it difficult because I'm your boss, or is it that you can't think of anything to say?"

Cameron asked me if it was "really okay to talk openly" about what he felt.

I looked at Jake who smiled and nodded yes. I grinned at Cameron while saying, "Sure, I'll protect you from him. What are you thinking?"

Then Cameron talked directly to me and avoided looking at Jake. "I like Jake. He's a good boss. But he is my boss and he has more power than I do. Power scares me when I'm dependent on someone who has more than I do."

Jake asked, "what would it take for you feel comfortable negotiating the details about how I provide support to you?"

Once again, Cameron expressed his concerns.

"This is all so new to me, I'm not sure how to answer. I don't want to say something that might make you irritated with me sometime in the future?"

Jake turned to me and asked, "Isn't what we're doing intended to protect employees from that kind of thing happening?"

I responded, "That's precisely the point!"

Jake continued, "You see, Cameron. I'm trying to stop supervising by always looking for things that I can point out for my employees to correct. I am trying to lead by always looking for ways to help you meet your commitments. Do you see what I'm trying to say?"

Cameron answered that he understood the idea. But, he added, "there's a big difference between talking about it and doing it."

Jack agreed and said, "I'm serious enough about this that I'm going to sign this sheet when we agree on what we want it to say. Are you willing to help me be a better leader?"

Only at that point was Cameron able to say, "When you put it that way, how can I refuse?"

This anecdote also illustrates the importance of the facilitator's role in implementation. The facilitator is viewed as an expert, a protector, and a mediator, who gives leaders and direct reports confidence to deal successfully with difficult and sensitive issues.

Signed support commitments protect direct reports from potential reprisals both in partnering meetings and in the long term. These commitments provide predetermined mutually desirable methods for generating and processing new ideas and resolving differences. As a meeting kickoff, the negotiating and signing of support commitments sets the example and mood for synergistic leader-direct-report relationships.

Seek Understanding

The guiding communication philosophy in negotiating is, "Seek first to understand and then to be understood." This philosophy is one of Stephen Covey's seven habits of highly effective people (1989). A leader implements this philosophy by inviting direct reports to read their expectations aloud and to give their interpretations *before* the leader says anything about his or her interpretations.

When direct reports read expectations aloud, it helps focus both the leader's and direct report's attention on the same thing, and the way they read—with hesitation or difficulty, mispronouncing words, or racing through—reveals much about how direct reports feel about expectations. It also focuses the resulting dialogue on mutual understanding. Leaders can discover perception or opinion differences and help their direct reports discuss and resolve them. Such a discussion goes a long way toward ensuring that leaders understand direct reports' perception of each expectation.

When reports read the expectations, leaders may discover that direct reports did not understand the meanings of some words. Such misunderstandings often create fear, uncertainty, and even anger. Discovering misinterpretations makes it simple for the leader to clarify what is meant. In addition, some people read poorly but have hidden it all their lives, especially from their supervisors. Discovering this problem makes it possible to assist them. Finally, direct reports sometimes interpret the meanings of words and sentences differently from the intended meanings. Discovering these errors makes it simple to eliminate destructive differences.

Start with Support Commitments

As suggested earlier, leaders should initiate negotiations by discussing their support commitments. This is a major paradigm shift for most supervisors. Joel Barker's videotape *Discovering the Future: The Business of Paradigms* (1989) is a very effective tool with which to start this activity. Barker explains paradigms, demonstrates how much they control our lives, and gives many familiar examples of how people can lose when they are reluctant to change destructive paradigms. Accepting the principle of leadership support is the biggest paradigm shift that most people must make in order to use employee partnering. The videotape sets the stage exceptionally well for leaders and direct reports to accomplish this shift.

Leaders and direct reports should discuss each leadership support commitment, agreeing on the words that fit best. They should also agree on how they both expect to accomplish their own part of each support item. Leaders should pencil in the changes and sign the support commitments sheet before they start discussing their reports' achievement expectations.

Negotiate Achievement Expectations

After signing the support page, the teams proceed to the achievement expectations, which the report reads aloud, as I described earlier. After a leader and an employee agree on the wording for the introductory paragraphs, they should discuss the levels of achievement they expect for each expectation's achievement statements. (See Exhibit 1.2 on p. 16.) The leader invites the direct report to give his or her wording, data, and rationales. This is where most empowerment occurs. The leader must want the employee to feel that he or she is in control of what he or she agrees to accomplish. The employee who feels in control will have a deep resolve to accomplish commitments.

The leader's negotiating challenge is to help direct reports clearly understand what achievement is realistic for each expectation in relation to each report's total job. Also, the leader must want to help reports think through their potential to accomplish the expectations. When leaders and reports set ambitious goals that direct reports can achieve, the achievement produces higher feelings of self-worth, greater self-motivation, and more customer satisfaction. Unrealistic goals that remain unachieved produce feelings of personal failure, which lead to demotivation and relationship problems. The following example illustrates how a leader can guide a direct report to set realistic goals. This particular leader, Kelly, was a department head in a manufacturing company. Kelly began by asking Ray, her direct report, what percentages he thought would "best describe excellent achievement" for a certain expectation.

Ray answered, "This one is really important, I always try to do it right."

"I know Ray, but think about it. Which ones of all of your expectations do you consciously try not to do right sometimes?"

"That doesn't make sense. I don't understand your question."

"I think I heard you say you always try to do this one right all the time. Correct?"

"Yes."

"Does that mean there are some of your expectations that you don't try every time to do right?"

"No! I never intentionally do less than the best possible. What I'm saying is that this expectation is really important."

"Do you have any expectations that are not important to do right at the time you are doing them?"

"Well, . . . no, but I don't consider them all equally important."

"Ah, but you see, importance is not the criterion we are talking about. We are working on a combination of what is realistic and challenging. Importance, in relation to expectations, tends to vary on the job with the pressures of the moment. What we are trying to describe is successful achievement for this expectation irrespective of importance."

"How can anyone do better than 100 percent?"

"Ray, have you ever been sick, had a splitting headache, been overwhelmed with distractions, been under severe stress, or been asked to accomplish an impossible task?"

"Sure, I think everybody has."

"Do those kinds of happenings cause you to make errors, miss deadlines, forget things that need to be done, or cause you to foul things up?"

"Sure, . . . unfortunately."

"Okay, so take all of those hindering conditions into account. Also, consider that you have twenty-four expectations to accomplish at an excellent level. What percent of the time that you do this expectation, during the next four months, can you do it perfectly?"

"I don't know. I never thought about it that way."

"Do you enjoy being successful?"

"Doesn't everyone?"

"Are you as successful as you would like to be?"

"I confess, I would like to be a lot more successful than I am."

"That's what I'm trying to do now is help you make success possible for yourself. To do that, we need to agree on a level of achievement that we both feel is excellent but realistic. I want the expectation to challenge you. But to succeed, you have to be able to accomplish whatever you commit to. Always thinking you should be perfect is a lose-lose proposition. We are defining win-win."

"Okay, then. Help me think through some numbers that are challenging and realistic."

Several techniques are important in this conversation. Kelly remained patient because she really wanted Ray to understand what an achievement agreement meant. She was willing to try several approaches until she found one that made sense to him. She preferred to pull ideas from him rather than to push ideas onto him, and she was realistic about what could be expected of him on this item. Above all, she kept Ray in control of his input to this expectation.

Discussing the rating numbers causes people to understand expectations in measurable terms. The numbers are not very important per se. They are more important as targets that inspire people to achieve a level of agreement. Working to agree on what the numbers mean causes leaders and direct reports to think creatively, rationally, and supportively.

Negotiate Specific Support

The last point of discussion on each expectation is the specific support the leader will supply for it. This support is additional to the general support described in the Leadership Support Commitments. To begin the negotiation, the leader asks the direct report, "What support will you need to accomplish this expectation at the level that we agreed upon in Excellent achievement statements a, b, c, and d?"

The leader must encourage the direct report to picture himself or herself accomplishing the expectation and to imagine any situation that might arise outside of his or her normal sphere of control. When the report describes a valid need for potential extra support, the leader should negotiate it on the spot and record it in the space provided on the expectation agreement form.

Many expectations will not require additional support. However, asking the question is a good problem prevention practice and reinforces the employee's new sense of empowerment.

There is no risk that support commitments made in this meeting will put leaders in a bind later. Instead, these commitments cause leaders to anticipate and prevent the problems the direct report foresees, rather than to wait until problems arise and then try to solve them. The act of determining where extra support is needed also empowers and guides direct reports to be part of the problem prevention process.

Offering additional support at this point of negotiating partnering agreements may appear more demanding to leaders than making traditional work assignments. But discussing and providing this support prevents so many problems that it is time well invested. It pays extraordinary dividends in higher efficiency, lower stress, and greater job satisfaction when compared to the results of traditional superior-subordinate transactions.

Some managers are concerned that they will not be able to get hard-nosed autocratic supervisors to make commitments to support their employees' work efforts. However, the partnering procedures themselves come to the rescue here. Partnering agreements are implemented from the top of the organization down. All supervisors, even hard-nosed autocrats, are invited to define and request support for their own achievement commitments before they experience being challenged to offer support for their employees. Because that first experience of negotiating their own support commitments with their leaders is satisfying and empowering rather than threatening to supervisors, they are usually comfortable with inviting their direct reports to request specific support.

Furthermore, all supervisory support is evaluated and discussed during the supervisors' own achievement reviews. When a supervisor's leadership expectation rates low, leadership will become the subject of a performance improvement plan for that supervisor.

Organizationwide negotiation of specific support commitments causes anticipating problems and making plans to be current practices at all management levels. Anticipating and planning are no longer just delegated (or dumped) downward, as is common in most supervisor-subordinate relationships.

A specific support negotiation that occurred between Julie, a medical quality assurance program officer, and her leader, Francis, who was the human resources director, illustrates how requests for support can produce needed planning at other organizational levels. Julie agreed to make sure 90 percent of all employees' agreements would have quality assurance expectations that met company quality assurance standards. Once Francis and Julie were comfortable with their agreement over the responsibility she would assume for quality assurance policies, procedures, and systems, Francis asked her what she needed from him "to feel certain" that she could achieve this expectation.

Because the new company policy required that all employees have support achievement agreements that included a quality assurance expectation, Julie felt she needed "some way to make sure the expectations will result in everyone's meeting the standards." Francis agreed that made sense and asked her what she had in mind.

She replied, "I was thinking of the company's adopting a companion policy to the one for agreements. We need something that would require the quality assurance officer to review and sign off on the quality assurance expectation in everyone's agreement. Also, I need some kind of budget for training when the team achievement evaluations identify employees who need training to improve their quality performance."

Again, Francis agreed this made sense; however, he could not provide this particular support himself. Therefore, he told Julie, "I can't give you a firm yes on the policy or an amount for the budget at the moment. I've got to negotiate this with my leader first. Right now, let's finish all the rest of these expectations. I'll have an answer for you on this one by a week from today? How's that?" And Julie agreed to that solution.

This exchange shows evidence of teamwork, employee involvement, leadership, employee initiative, problem anticipation and problem prevention, and empowerment. The approach is proactive, not reactive. Partnering procedures produced these results, which are examples of the kind of improvement referred to earlier when it was stated that partnering with employees makes ordinary improvement efforts up to seventy times more productive.

Rating Guide

The rating guide is a tool that helps leaders and their reports decide on valid and helpful achievement ratings. A customized guide is prepared for each expectation. First, leaders and their reports determine the percentage of achievement that will represent an excellent performance. Then a facilitator completes the guide, as part of the process of producing final versions of the agreements, containing the negotiated changes. The facilitator uses the percentage that the leader and the report selected as the median of a range of numbers in column three of the rating guide. (See Exhibit 1.4.) Once the "excellent" range is established, the facilitator can determine the ranges that will represent exceptional achievement, very low achievement, and moderate achievement. (See Table 1.1 on page 20).

Cosigning Partnering Agreements

The objective of cosigning leader–direct report partnering agreements is to maximize mutual commitment. When all support and achievement expectations have been negotiated, even though the changes are only written in, not typed, it is a good idea for leaders and direct reports to sign the signature page (Exhibit 1.6 on page 19) at this time because the signing may stimulate thoughts about additional changes that should be included in the final copy.

Kouzes and Posner (1987, p. 226) describe three fundamental criteria for total commitment: give people a sense of choice, make choices visible to others, and create choices that are hard to revoke.

When leaders and direct reports mutually sign their negotiated agreements, they make a choice to do so. The signing makes the choices visible to others. And mutually signed agreements are difficult to back out of or ignore. By signing their partnering agreements, leaders and their reports make the ultimate act of commitment to expectations and create the ultimate tool that empowers direct reports to be successful.

Asking direct reports to sign agreements motivates them to negotiate effectively and to consider agreement contents thoroughly. A reluctance to sign is an indicator of unsatisfied concerns that may one day disrupt work relationships. Those potential disruptions exist whether or not they are discovered early and prevented from becoming a reality.

Some skeptics of win-win leadership practices believe that some employees will acquiesce and sign almost anything they are asked to sign. However, even in such rare cases, acquiescent direct reports are likely to have had their potential concerns addressed during the negotiations of general leadership support, expectation and achievement levels, and specific support for each expectation. Furthermore, acquiescent employees' common fear of future reprisals is typically allayed by a leader's commitment, set forth in the leadership support agreement, to resolve differences through a facilitated discussion, to seek "win-win" resolutions, and to "hold no grudges." The presence of a facilitator also ensures that direct reports' interests are fairly considered.

Signed agreements do not, as some people fear, constrain either leaders or direct reports from changing expectations as needed. Both leaders and direct reports can renegotiate expectations anytime. In their support agreements, leaders commit to document new priorities and negotiate agreement adjustments whenever their expectations change. Putting changed expectations in writing reduces the whimsical and surprise expectation changes that are so common and destructive in ordinary work relationships.

The following example is a sample of the dialogue that can occur at the point of signing. After Quintin, a manufacturing company shift leader, and Al, his direct report, had finished negotiating their partnering agreement, Quintin signed it and offered it to Al to sign. But Al did not take the set of papers, which made Quintin uneasy. He asked Al if he was "uncomfortable" with signing the agreement.

Al said, "I'm not sure."

"You didn't take it when I gave it to you, so you must have some reluctance."

"I guess I do, but I can't tell exactly why."

"I'm not going to force you to sign this, but I do want to try to find out what's the hang up so we can resolve it."

"I know signing it is a good idea. It is just that it seems so final when you sign something."

"Apparently that feeling of finality bothers you."

"It makes me think of the old saying, 'signing your life away.' "

"Does it make you feel vulnerable?"

"Yeah. I think it does. Everything is so out in the open. Signing is the final step of a whole bunch of new things. It's all kind of overwhelming."

Quintin responded that he found Al's feelings "encouraging." When Al asked why, Quintin took the opportunity to explain that what they were working on was "mutual trust," because they had agreed on "mutual expectations to ensure each other's success." This helped Al to see that Quintin might "feel a little vulnerable committing to the support expectations."

Quintin agreed that he did, but he said, "When I think of what we've accomplished by doing this, the prospects of being vulnerable together seems like a plus not a minus."

"Okay, Al said, "give me that paper to sign. That's the way I see it too. I guess I just had to hear you say it for me to believe it."

Decreased Legal Risks

The threat of litigious relationships has been a primary reason for management to develop partnering between organizations. Relationship problems between employees and employers can be equally serious. The partnering Agreement Signature Page ties together all the partnering procedures that serve to eliminate the causes of employee-employer litigation.

The costly settlements that have occurred when employer organizations were sued and found not to have complied with their own documented, specific or implied policies are a direct result of win-lose cultures. Knowledge of these settlements has caused many organizations to refuse to put in writing or to sign anything that might be construed as an employee agreement. Not signing anything is wise in win-lose cultures. But the reverse is true in win-win cultures.

Employee partnering procedures are structured to eliminate or overcome the reasons that employees sue employers. Win-win partnering agreements and team achievement evaluations maximize employee empowerment, success, trust, and loyalty. The signature page states the intent of the entire system to foster cooperative bonds for the benefit of customers, employees, and employers. That statement reinforces and confirms the win-win intent of employee partnering, and it too is open to negotiation by leaders and direct reports.

As effective as employee partnering is, nothing can wholly prevent frivolous suits against employers. Therefore, paragraph three of the signature page must always be included as a disclaimer, so the agreement cannot be considered an employment contract. The form of this statement that is used in Exhibit 1.6 is the one that attorneys recommend for inclusion in all organizational employee relations documents, so leaders should not change the wording of this paragraph. It protects employers against frivolous suits, but does not diminish the win-win intent of partnering.

6

Using Achievement Evaluations to Support Continuous Improvement

Performance evaluations in ordinary work cultures are rarely satisfying to anyone. With partnering agreements in place, achievement evaluations are usually satisfying to all stakeholders, all those who have an interest in the results of evaluations.

The partnering evaluation objective is for leaders and direct reports to agree on the one or two expectations in which they most want to improve team achievement.

During implementation, the first leader-direct-report team achievement review is done about thirty days after the final partnering agreements are completed. After that, ongoing reviews ideally occur every four to six months. During reviews, leaders and direct-reports exchange their perceptions of how actual achievement compares to negotiated achievement. Thus, reviews automatically result in a discussion of the original terms of the agreements and a renegotiation of support and expectations where appropriate. The discussions also renew mutual leader-direct-report commitment to agreements for the next performance period, and the entire process supports the broader goal of synergistic relationships and continuous improvement.

Determining the Achievement Ratings

The initial rating activity occurs before the review meeting. Leaders rate a direct report's achievement by following the guidelines in the Review of Support and Achievement placed on the back of each expectation sheet. (See Exhibit 1.7 on page 20.) The numbers that define levels one through four will have been determined at the time of the original agreement. Initially, leaders reflect on their leadership support and their direct report's achievement of each expectation for the performance period just completed. They record just enough information in the leader's space, on the review guide to jog their memories during the discussions to follow. Direct reports do the same, recording their notes in the direct reports' space on their copy of the review guide.

To rate each expectation, leaders look at the expectation on the front side of the guide and read the first excellent achievement statement to refresh their understanding of the agreed achievement level. Leaders then return to the review guide and look at the four levels of percentage ranges for statement (a). They mark (*) the numbers that best describe their perception of the direct report's achievement compared to the achievement expectation described in statement (a). For example Exhibit 6.1 shows that 87 percent to 93 percent of the time the direct report would have achieved an excellent rating if he or she had fulfilled an expectation described in achievement statement (a). The leader has determined that the report fulfilled the expectation 81 percent of 86 percent of the time and the leader has starred that level-two entry. The leader also selected rating levels for achievement statements (b) and (c). Then the leader recorded the rating achievement levels in the blanks below the guide and averaged them to reach an overall achievement of 3 for this expectation.

When leaders and direct reports have completed their ratings for all expectations, they are to record them on their copies of the Table of Achievement Ratings. (See Table 1.2 on page 22.) This table lists all the achievement expectations that are in the agreement. They exchange with each other their sets of numbers at least two days before they get together to discuss them. When leaders and direct reports differ by three-tenths of a point or more or give a rating lower than 3 (excellent) for any expectation, that rating pinpoints an area of potential stress.

Prior to their review meeting, leaders and direct reports typically study the numbers and try to anticipate what they can do to improve achievement on low-rated expectations. Like the percentages agreed upon for the excellent achievement statements, the rating numbers are intended to generate mutually satisfying and productive communication. Selecting a numerical representation of a perceived achievement level causes leaders and direct reports to reflect back on actual occurrences during the review period. It leads them to think objectively and to develop a rationale for their rating selections.

That rationale will be the basis of discussion when perceptions of achievement are compared and differences resolved. The numbers are not grades or

Exhibit 6.1. Sample Rating Guide.

	1	2	3 Excellent	4
a.	75-80	81-86 *	87-93	94-100
b.	75-80	81-86	87-93 *	94-100
c.	86-89	90-93	94-96	97-100 *
d.	______	______	______	______

Rate achievement levels. On the basis of your notes and the percentages listed in the customized rating guide, rate the direct report's actual achievement levels (one, two, three, or four) for the achievement statements (a), (b), (c), and (d) that appear on the front of this sheet. Record the levels here: (a) 2 , (b) 3 , (c) 4 , (d) NA . Compute and record the average achievement rating: 3 .

reflections of employee worth. They do not even mean that the low performance they reflect is employees' fault. They serve only to simplify the process of identifying stress points that must be eliminated through an improvement plan.

The Review Meeting

Leaders should open reviews with a discussion of the higher-rated expectations. Exchanging positive feedback acknowledges and compliments real, specific, and mutual excellence; creates a natural synergy; and nurtures mutual feelings of self-worth. This procedure causes individuals to look forward to performance reviews because each review always progresses on a positive and rewarding track. As the old song title says, "Accentuate the Positive and Eliminate the Negative."

After dialogue is complete on all expectations rated three or above, the lower ratings and rating differences are discussed. This is not a shift in focus from good to bad. It is a shift from discussing excellent achievement to analyzing where the team should put its effort to most effectively improve the work relationship and team achievement.

By the time a leader and direct report are ready to discuss the low-rated expectations, they have shown integrity and built up their egos and self-worth. They have added to the "P/PC (production/production capability) Balance," or emotional bank account, of which Stephen Covey (1989) speaks. They will improve their achievement and increase their capability of improving even more because of the synergy of their relationship. Moreover, in my experience, discussions on all expectations, regardless of rating, produce important insights and improvements.

Comparing rating numbers makes it easy to determine key stress points. On Table 1.2, for example, the ratings for expectation twelve show seven-tenths of a point difference. This is a major difference in perceptions of accomplishment, yet the leader's rating itself (only one-tenth of a point under 3) indicates very little dissatisfaction for expectation twelve. Expectation seven shows a much greater problem because, even though the leader and the report agree on 2.6, that rating is four-tenths of a point below three and indicates serious mutual dissatisfaction. The leader-direct-report team stands to gain more from improving achievement on number seven rather than on number 12.

Finally, as leaders and reports compare achievement perceptions, they complete the paradigm shift from win-lose to win-win that partnering implementation began.

The next example shows how leaders may have to refocus employees' perceptions about review ratings. Jack, a company president, has exceptionally good rapport with his people and jokes easily with them. When he and his four direct reports met to compare ratings during their first team achievement review, Jack's ratings turned out to be similar to the direct reports' ratings. On some expectations, he rated their achievement higher than they rated it. But one direct report, Sam, was a proud and argumentative individual, and he haggled with

Jack about some of Jack's minimally lower ratings. No difference was too small to challenge. After Sam challenged a lower rating for the fifth time, Jack asked, "Why does two or three tenths of a percentage point torque you so tight?"

Sam replied, "Doesn't everyone want to get the highest rating they can get?"

Jack grinned broadly, leaned toward Sam and said, "You may be smart, but you don't get it do you?"

Sam shot back, "What's so dumb about getting the highest possible rating, that's how you win where I come from."

"So, if I give you a higher score and you get the overall highest score of all four of you, what do you win?"

". . . I win the argument with you!"

"What bank will take that for a deposit?"

After everyone had a good chuckle out of the sparring match, Sam became serious again. "My whole life has been playing to win. So what's the new game?"

Jack looked to me to answer Sam. From my work with the group for several months, I knew that Sam listened to Alan more than to any of the others. I pointed at Alan, who had demonstrated a good grasp of the concepts, and Jack asked Alan to explain what the review was designed to accomplish. When Alan asked why he had been chosen to do this, Jack said, " 'Cause you know what's going on and you're the only one he listens to."

Alan looked at Sam and said, "This is not a contest. We aren't competing with each other. We're not being graded. These numbers by themselves mean nothing. When we compare them with Jack's numbers, they tell us where to concentrate to improve our performance."

When Jack asked Sam what he thought now, Sam said, "It sure is different. I think I'll be like Mikey. I think I'm going to like it."

Jack and I have talked several times about that dialogue. We agree that what we witnessed was a spectacular shift in thinking for those four upper- level managers. Though the shift from win-lose to win-win thinking may not always be as visible in all employees, an achievement evaluation using this system is a profound and satisfying experience for most people.

Although Jack loved to banter as much as anyone, and he did so, he followed the win-win guidance style, of leading rather than pushing. He led by asking questions that caused Sam to discover profound insight. He invited and empowered others to help him search for ways to connect with Sam's concerns. He never became defensive. Throughout the meeting, the direct reports were in control of and comfortable with what they wanted to say.

Determining Causes of Low Achievement

One objective for leaders and direct reports conducting a review is to identify the remedies for low achievement. Once the causes of low achievement are understood, it is simple to select or create appropriate remedies to eliminate them. As illustrated in Chapter One, in addition to a ratings section, the back of each achievement expectation has a section to help leaders and their reports agree on causes of performance shortcomings. (See Exhibit 1.7 on page 20.) As leaders and reports identify shortcomings, it is important for them to avoid discussing each other as the source of shortcomings; individuals need only acknowledge and understand the shortcomings to agree on a remedy for them.

As I described earlier, the four causes of low achievement are insufficient understanding or support, insufficient knowledge or skill, insufficient capability, and insufficient commitment.

To determine shortcomings, leader-direct-report teams consider the four causes as questions. They address the cause questions in the order that they appear, so that they look first at the simplest cause, misunderstanding or support shortcomings. Looking at this cause first also helps leaders empower direct reports to contribute effectively.

A leader starts discussion on the first cause with this statement: "Up to now, I have thought we both understood this expectation the same way. Maybe we don't. Please explain again your interpretation of this expectation and your feelings about the excellent levels of achievement." After the discussion of this point, the leader says, "I need to know what additional support might have been useful to you in achieving this expectation." Leaders must listen carefully to understand both ideas and feelings. This is a fruitful time to improve work relationships.

The process of discussing understanding and support is the same as the original process of negotiating the expectation. If lack of information or support turns out to be a cause, it is checked off on the form. In the comments section, the leader notes key points to address in the improvement plan. When possible, the team resolves misunderstandings and lack of support at the review meeting, not later.

Exhibit 6.2 shows the front side of an expanded checklist for determining causes. The checklist includes follow-up statements to narrow the range of each cause and is especially effective for out-of-the-ordinary performance review discussions, such as those about critical incidents that may result in discipline or termination.

When discussion—with or without the checklist—is complete on cause one, the team considers cause two the same way. The leader can start discussion of insufficient knowledge or skill with this question: "What can you think of that might indicate insufficient knowledge or skill as a cause for the low achievement?" If the response suggests knowledge or skill may be lacking, the team discusses and clarifies the knowledge or skill needed. If direct reports have ever in the past performed the expectation adequately, the cause of a low rating is probably not lack of knowledge or skill.

When discussion is complete on cause two, the team considers cause three the same way. Leaders can start discussion on insufficient capability with the question. "What can you think of that might indicate lack of capability?" When

Exhibit 6.2. Low-Achievement Checklist.

Leader ______________________ Title ______________ Date __________

Direct Report ______________________ Title ______________ Date __________

Review is for: Regular achievement review ____ Critical incident ____

Expectation under review: ______________________________________

Situation summary: ______________________________________

____

____

Leader, study the checklist in relation to direct reports' achievement of the expectation. Discuss each cause in sequence with direct report, to agree which one (or more) applies to the expectation.

Cause one: not sufficiently informed of expectations or not sufficiently supported.

1. Written company policy does not exist for, or does not adequately specify, the achievement expectation, so that direct report can accomplish it.
2. Appropriate policy and performance standards exist but have not been formally discussed with direct report.
3. Sufficient information to accomplish this expectation has not been given to direct report.
4. Existing company or leader practices inhibit direct report from accomplishing this expectation.
5. Resources such as lead time, material, equipment, other people, procedures, decisions, and so forth that are beyond direct report's control were insufficient for direct report to accomplish this expectation.

Cause two: not sufficiently trained. Direct report does not have sufficient knowledge or skill to accomplish this expectation.

Cause three: not sufficiently capable. Direct report has a mental or physical limitation that prevents him or her from having the potential to learn to accomplish this expectation.

Cause four: not sufficiently committed.

1. Direct report is not convinced this expectation is important enough to accomplish it as expected and allows other things to distract from achievement of this expectation.
2. Confrontations are a common part of this expectation. Direct report is uncomfortable with confrontation to the point that he or she avoids achieving this expectation.
3. Direct report disagrees with this performance expectation.

none of the first three causes is producing the lack of achievement, then lack of commitment has to be the cause.

After the leader and direct report have discussed all four causes for each low-rated expectation, they decide which one or two achievement expectations to include in their improvement plans and proceed to develop those plans.

Only one or two expectations should be selected because most people cannot stay focused on more than one or two major improvement efforts at one time. The effort is compounded for leaders, who may have, for instance, six direct reports and consequently be partners in six improvement plans with up to twelve expectations to work on concurrently. Leaders also have their own performance improvement plan. One or two expectations per improvement plan is realistic, more than that is not.

Preparing Improvement Plans

The objective of an improvement plan is to spell out specific assignments, support commitments, and learning experiences that will eliminate the known causes of achievement shortcomings, no matter who is responsible for them. The first three potential causes are leadership shortcomings and the fourth is direct reports' shortcomings. The message is that leaders and direct reports both have shortcomings. Leaders must want to eliminate causes, not point fingers of blame.

Leader-direct-report teams negotiate improvement plans in the same manner as the agreement expectations. The agreement draft should include a form (Exhibit 6.3) to assist in plan preparation.

Exhibit 6.4 is a checklist of general remedies for each of the four causes. When the cause is lack of information, the remedy is usually additional communication. Teams can resolve that kind of shortcoming on the spot. They can also negotiate additional support on the spot. In some situations, it may take time to confirm availability of additional support. Even so, leaders should document what they and their reports mutually decided about that additional support, on the principle that what gets written gets remembered.

Insufficient knowledge or skill is the cause that usually requires the most detailed plan to improve relationships and team achievement. Remedies for this cause could be a series of work assignments, training or education, mentoring or shadowing, or home study.

Insufficient capability does not appear often, but it can be perplexing when it does. Generally, leaders should seek guidance from their leaders to discuss this cause of low achievement. Solutions could call for a change in job responsibilities, a total change of jobs, a transfer, a termination, or other considerations. Many of these choices are beyond most leaders' authority to decide on their own.

Insufficient commitment is a complex cause of low achievement. Many organizational leaders commonly lament that their biggest employee problem is that some employees do not care whether they do a good job or not. The only thing they seem concerned about is picking up their paychecks on time. Without partnering agreements in place, organizations have no means to influence and change that uncommitted attitude. The uncommitted person can be terminated, but leaders have no assurance that the replacement will be any better. Furthermore, a replacement may not be available.

When leaders address this cause, they can legitimately say that responsibility for lack of commitment belongs to direct reports themselves. It is the only cause of low achievement for which an effort to motivate employees is an appropriate remedy.

A leader initially addresses lack of commitment by saying to the report,

Exhibit 6.3. Team Performance Improvement Plan Outline.

Direct Report ______________________ Title ____________ Date __________

Leader ___________________________ Title ____________ Date __________

Review is for: Regular achievement review ___ Critical incident ___

Expectation in question: ____

Situation summary: ____

____

____

Cause(s) of this low achievement: _____________________________________

Direct report's plan to improve performance of this expectation: ___________

____

____

____

____

____

____

____

____

____

____

Leader's plan to improve performance of this expectation: _________________

____

____

____

____

____

____

____

____

____

"Our discussion shows that you clearly understand my expectations and that you have willingly agreed to them. I have provided all the support that we negotiated for you to achieve this expectation. However, for reasons that only you can know and that are under your control, you are not achieving this expectation as you agreed. What will it take for you to achieve your commitment to this expectation?" The leader should be sure not to answer his or her own question but to listen to the direct report's candid response.

Exhibit 6.4. Low-Achievement Remedies Checklist.

Leader, remedies are provided for each low-achievement cause. Once you and your direct report agree on the appropriate cause, select the corresponding remedy. Use it as a guide to prepare a plan for improving achievement of the expectation.

Remedy for cause one: not sufficiently informed or supported.

1. Prepare a company policy manual for all major operations. As a more immediate response, prepare a set of written policies that support direct report's job expectations.
2. Negotiate a partnering agreement with direct report that includes the excellent achievement of this expectation. During negotiation of the partnering agreement, discuss the following:
   a. Company policy related to this expectation.
   b. Inhibiting practices. Negotiate support and/or change in the inhibiting practices.
   c. Negotiate a plan to provide adequate support and resources or to change the achievement expectations.

Remedy for cause two: not sufficiently trained. Select relevant training for direct report.

Remedy for cause three: not sufficiently capable. Reevaluate direct report and the expectation in order to change achievement expectations or recommend personnel position changes.

Remedy for cause four: not sufficiently committed. Explain to direct report that the discussion of causes to this point has established that he or she has sufficient understanding, support, knowledge, skill, and capability to achieve this expectation. The only rational conclusion is that he or she is not performing the expectation as expected for some reason that he or she has the potential to control. Explain that, in effect, he or she has not been sufficiently committed to accomplish the expectation as agreed. Allow for response and discuss the response. Then ask direct report, "What will it take for you to achieve this expectation the way you have agreed?" If there are no conditions offered, or none with the potential for a successfully negotiated resolution, in effect, direct report has chosen to be terminated for cause.

Summary of the action plan mutually worked out to improve performance of the expectation, or summary of the decision that will lead to termination: ______________

____

____

____

This leadership question transfers responsibility for lack of commitment to a direct report, but the question is not adversarial or coercive. The direct question simply makes it difficult for employees to remain resistant or passive in discussions to change behavior. The question provides nothing for them to resist. Also, direct reports are accustomed to the question because it is the same one the leader asks when the leader and the report consider the support needed to achieve each expectation. It leads the conversation directly to the point that needs to be resolved, it will produce a resolution that is mutually fair, and it allows a leader to be in control without controlling. In other words, asking this question and listening carefully to the answer is real leadership performance.

The leader may accept, reject, or negotiate an alternative to the direct report's answer. The leader can also consider the subcauses listed in the Low

Achievement Cause Checklist (Exhibit 6.2). These subcauses can suggest additional questions to clarify understanding and confirm that lack of commitment is the cause of the low achievement.

Leaders and direct reports often start discussing remedies to causes the moment they discover them. However, they are strongly advised not to address remedies until they have discussed all four potential causes of low achievement. At this point, they will have a better perspective on the report's achievement and will be able to produce more effective plans.

Traditional motivational programs focus on motivational theory. Knowing the theory supposedly improves leaders' psychoanalytical ability to discover employees' motivational hot buttons. That approach has little potential to achieve productive results. Employee partnering procedures address lack of employee commitment far more effectively than ordinary motivational programs for the following reasons:

- All partnering transactions empower direct reports for self-motivation.
- Lack of commitment is mutually confirmed to be the primary cause of low achievement. The employee acknowledges the shortcoming.
- The question, "What will it take. . . ?" is empowering rather than intimidating.
- In reply to a direct report's answer, leaders can accept, reject, or negotiate the answer.
- Responsibility for lack of commitment is transferred to direct reports.
- Leaders are in control without controlling direct reports.
- Employees are placed in control of themselves.
- The procedures produce win-win results.

After a leader and a direct report have selected the expectations and the related causes for which to prepare team improvement plans, determined the remedies that will eliminate the shortcomings, and planned and documented the actions needed to accomplish the remedies, they must also agree on how and when to measure the results of the plan efforts. They spell out what each of them expects of the other, and they cosign the improvement plan just as they did the agreement.

Leaders should encourage their direct reports to take as much initiative as possible to document and make the plan successful, and leaders should commit to supporting this plan in the same way that they support direct reports in achieving other expectations. The review procedure is a safe and simple way for leaders and direct reports to deal constructively with any problems or mutual differences.

7

Other Applications of Partnering Agreements

This chapter describes leadership partnering procedures that only some leaders must perform. These procedures concern unilateral personnel decisions, terminations, achievement-based compensation, and interviewing and hiring.

Procedures for Adverse Personnel Actions

The partnering objective in handling adverse personnel actions is to achieve the best possible results for the employees, leaders, and organizations affected by these actions.

To accomplish this objective, leaders need to help employees adjust quickly and productively when they are forced to change jobs internally, and minimize any basis that could support employee charges against the employer for terminating them.

Job Changes

Employees bumped out of one job and into another often experience morale problems. The leadership challenge is to help all involved parties establish win-win relationships in their new jobs and improve employee morale as quickly as possible. When an employee must change jobs and there are several jobs open, leaders for vacant positions (not the employee's supervisor) can prepare agreement drafts for those jobs and make the drafts available to all interested parties. The employees to be moved can then discuss these drafts with their current leader.

This discussion is not a negotiation but a focused dialogue with a trusted leader on the new jobs' specific expectations. Such a discussion will help employees get ready for the change and make wiser choices, insofar as they have choices.

Discipline or Termination

Of the four causes of low achievement, lack of commitment is the only one for which discipline or termination is an appropriate remedy. In the partnering philosophy, both employee and employer interests are to be considered in relation to discipline and termination. As human beings, employees deserve fair treatment and the support needed to succeed in their jobs. Moreover, the cost of employee turnover and of training replacements is very high. It does not pay to make hasty and potentially inappropriate disciplinary or termination decisions. Finally, because supervisory shortcomings are the cause of 99 percent of persistent low achievement, employees clearly deserve the benefit of the doubt when discipline or termination for low achievement is being considered.

I do not mean to intimidate leaders or discourage them from taking appropriate disciplinary action. However, through partnering procedures, leaders can discipline or terminate employees in a manner beneficial to all parties in the long term.

The first objective of disciplinary action should be to influence performance improvement. When that objective is not practical, or the employee noncompliance warrants immediate termination, the objective becomes to remove the person from the company at the least short- and long-term cost.

Disciplinary actions are usually responses to repeated unacceptable behavior that does not warrant termination for one offense. Or they may be responses to incidents of behavior prohibited by company policy: for example, theft, fighting, or drinking or being drunk on the job. Disciplinary actions call for precise and repeated application of the performance improvement procedures described in Chapter Six. The Appendix contains an example of brief yet effective documentation of progressive disciplinary actions using the Low-Achievement Cause Checklist and the Low-Achievement Remedies Checklist.

Terminations in the partnering system are simple and anticlimactic. They happen as a result of employees' repeatedly failing to achieve expectations that they thoroughly understood, willingly agreed to accomplish, and had sufficient support to achieve. This failure is unequivocal grounds for termination.

When employees must be terminated, employee partnering agreement procedures address the basic considerations of fairness to employees and good human relations in these ways:

- Leaders clarify expectations for employees, confirm employees' understanding of expectations, and support these expectations.
- Leaders confirm employee commitment to expectations and employee confidence to achieve as expected.
- Leaders continuously seek to provide additional support.
- Leaders base remedies for low achievement on actual causes, including leaders' own shortcomings.

The procedures also address the need to manage company risk:

- They are efficient, nonadversarial, and require minimum attorney's fees.
- They reduce legal risks.

- They reduce the guilt that leaders commonly feel when they terminate employees.
- They rescue most salvageable employees, which reduces turnover costs.

Supporting Achievement-Based Compensation

The objective of supporting achievement-based compensation is to have a valid evaluation system that supports synergistic leader–direct-report relationships and continuous performance improvement.

Achievement-based compensation is a new form of performance-based compensation and pay for performance. It is new in that it is based on actual employee accomplishment of negotiated excellent achievement expectations. Most pay-for-performance employee evaluations are based on generic performance standards that do not relate to individual achievement, are rarely negotiated with employees, and are rarely objectively quantified. For these reasons, the standards do not support pay for performance.

Once employee partnering agreements are in place, organizations can implement achievement-based compensation any time they choose without changing any part of the agreements. The only difference is that achievement ratings are used for the additional purpose of determining compensation. The basic procedure plugs the combined average rating from a review into a simple formula to compute compensation adjustments. The rating table shown in Table 1.1 is expanded by three columns as shown in Table 7.1, and information from that table is used in the formula shown at the foot of the table.

To adjust compensation on the basis of achievement, an organization must determine the base amount that each job is worth, and how much employees' achievement is worth compared to the base amount for their jobs. I suggest that direct reports' current pay be used as their base amount. For vacant jobs, organizations often determine job worth by surveying comparable compensation in other organizations. (Most organizations do this from time to time anyway, to adjust wages and salaries for cost-of-living changes.)

Achievement-based compensation rests on two premises. First, excellent achievement earns the base amount. Excellent achievement is accomplished when an employee's combined average rating for all areas of responsibility is 3. Second, when the average of all the achievement ratings exceeds excellent, is higher than 3, compensation is proportionately more than the base amount. Achievement that is less than excellent, less than 3, is worth proportionately less. Partnering procedures make it simple to determine the relative worth of employee achievement compared to the base amount.

As the first step each leader–direct-report team agrees on fair and mutually acceptable overall achievement ratings to be recorded in the final-rating column of the team's rating table. When the numbers in the leader-rating and direct-report-rating columns are the same concurrence already exists. When ratings differ by half a point (0.5) or less, the highest of the two numbers is used for the

Table 7.1 Rating Table for Computing Achievement Based Compensation.

	Expectations for Construction Foreman	*Performance Review Ratings*		*Achievement Compensation*		
		Leader's rating	*Direct report's rating*	*Agreed rating*	*Mediated rating*	*Final rating*
1	Communication	3.0	3.0			3.0
2	Policies and procedures	3.4	3.0			3.4
3	Safety and housekeeping	1.3	2.0		1.7	1.7
4	Cost-effective systems	2.9	2.8			2.9
5	Team productivity	3.3	3.0			3.3
6	Employee input job issues	3.4	3.0			3.4
7	Relations with other trades	2.6	2.6			2.6
8	Craftsperson training	3.3	3.0			3.3
9	Hiring and disciplining employees	3.0	2.6			3.0
10	Reporting labor costs	3.0	2.6			3.0
11	Requesting resources	3.3	2.6	3.1		3.1
12	Reporting	2.9	3.6		3.4	3.4
13	Drafting support and achievement expectations	3.0	3.0			3.0
14	Negotiating support and achievement expectations	3.0	2.6			3.0
15	Cosigning support and achievement expectations	3.4	3.2			3.4
16	Conducting team achievement reviews	3.1	3.7	3.6		3.6
17	Determining causes of shortcomings	3.0	3.0			3.0
18	Preparing improvement plans	3.0	3.0			3.0
19	Negotiating acceptance adverse actions	3.2	3.5			3.5
20	Supporting achievement-based compensation	2.7	3.4		2.9	2.9
21	Interviewing and evaluating job applications	3.6	3.6			3.6
	Total Expectations (TE) 21			Total Points (TP)		65.1

Note:
(TP) ÷ (TE) = combined average. Example: 65.1 ÷ 21 = 3.1
Combined average ÷ 3 = percent Example 3.1 ÷ 3 = 1.033
Percent X current hourly base amount = adjusted hourly wage
Example 1.03 × $10 per hour = $10.33 hourly wage

final rating. (The variance can be anything an organization chooses, but it should be the same for all employees in an organization.) This procedure favors direct reports and usually benefits the team and the employer, also, because it builds employee trust, loyalty, and resolve to achieve excellence.

When ratings vary by more than half a point, leaders and direct reports revisit their perceptions to resolve the differences to within half a point. Ratings arrived at in this manner are recorded in the agreed-ratings and final-ratings columns. (See expectations eleven and sixteen in Table 7.1.)

When a team is unable to agree on a rating, the team leader's leader is asked to help the team compare perceptions of the unresolved differences. If necessary, that leader will mediate a final number for unresolved ratings. In mediated sessions, all expectations are open for discussion, but only unresolved numbers are subject to change. The mediated final numbers should be no higher or lower than either team member's original ratings. Mediated ratings are recorded in the mediated-ratings and final-ratings columns. The final ratings are totaled and divided by the total number of expectations to produce a combined average. The combined average for the example in Table 7.1 is 3.1 (65.1 ÷ 21).

The value of the proportionate amount actual achievement is above or below excellent can be computed by any factor that a company chooses. The example in Table 7.1 uses a simple percentage factor. It is based on a maximum compensation of 133 percent of base pay for a perfect average rating of 4. There is no theoretical minimum. The example shows an average rating of 3.1. It produces a factor of 1.033. Given base pay of $10 per hour, the factor produces a 3.3 percent increase, resulting in an hourly rate of $10.33.

As an example for computing salaried compensation, assume that a person's rating average is the maximum, 4. 4 ÷ 3 = 1.333, for a maximum of 33.3 percent increase. If the base salary is $20,000, it would be multiplied by 1.333 for an annual salary of $26,667.

On a straight percentage basis, each tenth of a rating point is worth a 3.3 percent increase or decrease. An organization can use any factor in place of the 3.3 percent.

In pure applications of achievement-based compensation, average achievement that is less than excellent receives less than the base amount of compensation. Mistrust between management and labor (supervisors and employees) has been so serious for so long, however, that some companies implementing achievement-based compensation are reluctant to consider paying employees less than the base amounts when their achievement is below 3. I do not advocate this practice because of the history of management taking unfair advantage of employees in such situations. However, my experience with achievement-based compensation supports paying people what fair evaluations indicate they have earned, even when the amount is less than the base amount. When employees believe that expectations and evaluations are fair, most prefer compensation on the basis of how actual achievement compares to committed achievement, even when their accomplishments are below their commitments.

An illustration of this occurred in a company in which all jobs had a specified value. If their performance ratings averaged out to a 3, employees would receive the specified full amount for the next year. For a rating higher than 3, they would receive a proportionately higher amount, and for a rating below 3, their compensation would be proportionately lower.

Pam's rating was significantly below 3. Her leader, Justin, was concerned about it because he knew Pam had filed discrimination charges against a previous employer. Justin felt strongly that he had done everything he could to be clear on expectations and had provided the negotiated support so Pam could achieve the commitments in their agreement.

Justin was surprised and relieved when Pam said, "I'm disappointed in what I accomplished, but I don't blame you for my low ratings. At least I know what went wrong. I know what I have to do to get a better rating in the future and that I can count on your help. All I can hope for is a fair chance. I'm anxious to start improving."

Most employees appear willing to accept lower-than-expected compensation temporarily, when their low achievement warrants it, as long as they understand what they need to do to receive higher pay in the future. They also make it clear that they expect their companies to follow through with commitments to compensate them at a higher rate when the employees do achieve at higher levels. Those who work at eliminating personal shortcomings nearly always improve the worth of their achievement.

Partnering supports achievement-based compensation in the following ways:

- Achievement ratings are based on mutually agreed-upon objective expectations and evaluation criteria. Unrealistically high or low ratings by leaders or direct reports are unlikely. A leader's leader can ask for and evaluate the perceptions of performance that support the ratings.
- Intentional rating bias by leaders or direct reports is minimal. Initial ratings are supported with objective descriptions of actual happenings that can be verified or corrected by the leader's leader.
- Direct reports are protected from their leader's potentially unfair ratings. The leader's leader has the final say on any rating points not resolved by leaders and direct reports.
- Direct-report compensation is not adversely affected by leader shortcomings.
- Partnering procedures are philosophically and legally fair to employees, leaders, and employers. Leaders who follow them are not likely to be accused of being unfair.
- The leaders' leader can study the ratings and coach the team to resolve rating differences during a compensation review meeting.
- Management retains final control of compensation determination, but the final decision is nonstressful. Results nearly always benefit both employer and direct reports.
- Compensation is directly related to direct reports' real achievement.
- Leaders' performance in evaluating and rating direct reports' achievement is reviewed as part of the leaders' own leadership achievement evaluations.
- All aspects of this practice enhance work relationships.

Achievement-Based Bonuses

Bonuses are discretionary compensation for company employees over salary or wages. With partnering procedures in operation, achievement-based bonuses can benefit both employees and employers. For a successful achievement-based bonus program, the conditions under which bonuses will be paid must be established and publicized to all employees before the start of the first production period for which bonuses will be paid. For example, it could be established that a certain percentage of company net profits after taxes would go into a bonus pool and that bonus distribution would be limited to pool funds. All employees, except those prohibited by their labor contracts, could be eligible for the bonuses. All employees who worked for the full production period before a distribution should receive a portion of the bonus distribution. And a bonus amount should be the portion of the total bonus pool that the employee's salary is of the total payroll, adjusted by the employee's average achievement rating.

Such a system of procedures can work with or be separate from achievement-based compensation. Partnering procedures support both incentive programs equally well.

Achievement-based bonuses are computed from rating averages, as described for achievement-based compensation. Tables 7.2 and 7.3 illustrate two ways to determine bonus distribution. One way is to allocate a proportionate percentage of the bonus pool dollars to each salary range or job title. (Table 7.2). This works well when there is more than one person per job title. In Table 7.2, column one lists employees within each salary range and column two lists individual and group salaries. Column three lists the proportion that each person's salary is of the total payroll. It also shows the proportion that each individual's and each group's total is of the total payroll. Column four computes the dollar amount each group will receive from the total bonus. In this case, each group's share of the bonus is the same as its share of the payroll.

Column five contains each employee's average achievement rating from his or her Table of Ratings. This column also shows the total of the group ratings, which is used in column six to compute the proportion that each person's rating average is of the group average. Column seven is the dollar amount of the individual distribution, computed by multiplying column six by the dollar amount of the group's portion bonus pool, shown in column four.

Another way to decide bonus portions is to compute each person's portion individually. This variation works the same way whether one or several individuals hold a common job. Table 7.3 shows a combination of both methods. In this table, superintendent is the only job title with more than one person. Individual bonuses in Table 7.3 are computed the same way as bonuses for job groups in Table 7.2. The significant difference in the two examples is column six. In Table 7.3, column six shows each employee's bonus adjustment factor, which is derived from the employee's average rating divided by three. The bonus amount

Table 7.2. Achievement-Based Bonus Distribution for Salary-Range Groups.

Salary-Range Groups ($)	*Individual Salaries and Group Portions of Total Payroll ($)*	*Individual and Group Portions of Total Company Payroll*	*Group Portions of $60,000 Bonus Pool*	*Individual and Group Achievement Averages*	*Individual Portions of Group Bonus Pool*	*Bonus Paid ($)*
30,001–35,000						
Jerry	35,000	.0653	$11,418	3.1	.3334	3,807
Sara	34,000	.0634	(.1902 of $60,000)	3.3	.3548	4,051
Pete	33,000	.0616		2.9	.3118	3,560
Total	102,000	.1903		9.3	1.0000	11,418
28,000–30,000						
Earl	30,000	.0560	$13,206	3.0	.2381	3,144
Jerome	29,500	.0550	(.2201 of $60,000)	3.0	.2381	3,144
Harry	29,500	.0550		3.2	.2540	3,354
Eli	29,000	.0541		3.4	.2698	3,563
Total	118,000	.2201		12.6	1.0000	13,205
15,001–18,000						
Raymond	28,000	.0522	$21,150	2.9	.1355	2,866
Ansel	28,000	.0522	(.3525 of $60,000)	3.0	.1402	2,965
Margaret	28,000	.0522		3.2	.1495	3,162
Caley	27,000	.0504		3.1	.1449	3,065
Jose	26,000	.0485		3.0	.1402	2,965
Bobby	26,000	.0485		3.3	.1542	3,261
Ted	26,000	.0485		2.9	.1355	2,866
Total	189,000	.3525		21.4	1.0000	21,150

14,001–15,000						
Betty	15,000	.0280	$8,292	3.0	.1961	1,626
Carla	15,000	.0280	(.1382 of $$60,000)	3.3	.2157	1,789
Tim	15,000	.0280		3.1	.2026	1,680
Carlos	14,500	.0271		2.9	.1895	1,571
Kim	14,500	.0271		3.0	.1961	1,626
Total	74,000	.1382		15.3	1.0000	8,292
Up to 14,000						
Paula	14,000	.0261	$5,934	3.0	.2419	1,435
Rachel	13,000	.0242	(.0989 of $60,000)	3.1	.2500	1,484
Aiko	13,000	.0243		3.4	.2742	1,627
Jan	13,000	.0243		2.9	.2339	1,388
Total	53,000	.0989		12.4	1.0000	5,934
	Total payroll: $536,000	1.0000				Total bonuses paid: $59,999

Table 7.3. Achievement-Based Bonus Distribution for Individuals/Job Titles.

Individuals/ Job Titles	*Salaries ($)*	*Individual and Group Portions of Total Payroll*	*Individual and Group Portions of $25,000 Bonus Pool*	*Achievement Average Rating*	*Bonus Adjustment Factor*	*Bonus Paid ($)*
VP operations	48,000	.1708	$4,270 (.1708 of $25,000)	3.1	3.1 ÷ 3 = 1.03	4,398
Estimator	41,000	.1459	$3,648 (.1459 of $25,000)	3.2	3.2 ÷ 3 = 1.07	3,903
Project manager	44,000	.1566	$3,915 (.1566 of $25,000)	2.9	2.9 ÷ 3 = 0.97	3,798
Superintendent 1	39,000	.1388	$9,788 (.3915 of $25,000)	2.9	.3187	3,120
Superintendent 2	36,000	.1281		3.2	.3516	3,441
Superintendent 3	35,000	.1246		3.0	.3297	3,227
		.3915		9.1	1.0000	9,788
Office manager	22,000	.0783	$1,958 (.0783 of $25,000)	3.2	3.2 ÷ 3 = 1.07	2,095
Clerk	16,000	.0569	$1,423 (.0569 of $25,000)	2.8	2.8 ÷ 3 = 0.93	1,323
	Total payroll $281,000	1.0000				Total bonuses paid $25,305

in column four is multiplied by that factor to determine the dollar amount in column six.

This method usually results in a total bonus amount that is slightly different than the starting bonus pool amount; however, the difference is rarely significant. In Table 7.3, for example, the difference is $302.

Interviewing and Evaluating Job Applicants

The objective of this expectation is to simplify employment interviews, assure selection of the most qualified candidate, and hire employees into partnering agreements.

Interviewing is the art of asking the right questions and doing it effectively. Nonprofessional interviewers often spend too much time explaining and promoting jobs and not enough time learning about applicants' capability. Partnering procedures solve that problem.

In preparation for their job interviews, job applicants study a draft of an expectation agreement draft for the vacant job. During the interview, the applicants are asked to interpret the partnering agreement expectations and describe their capabilities in relation to the expectations. This procedure reveals the ways applicants see themselves accomplishing jobs. When an applicant is hired, the job leader and the new hire (now direct report) negotiate and finalize the agreement.

Partnering procedures can be used alone or with other criteria to ascertain and then compare applicant qualifications. The procedures are equally effective for new hires and promotions.

Antidiscrimination laws and regulations prohibit interviewers from asking questions irrelevant to applicants' abilities to accomplish job expectations. Using an expectation agreement draft as the basis for interview questions eliminates these prohibited questions. An interview built around job expectations produces results that benefit employers and satisfy Equal Employment Opportunity regulations.

Agreement drafts can be used in preliminary as well as final interviews with applicants who have already passed a screening interview or, at least, an application screening. Due to the thoroughness of partnering-based interviews, I recommend them only for short-listed applicants.

Job applicants should be provided copies of the drafts at least a day before the interview. Drafts used for this purpose have the excellent achievement statements completed, so applicants can study the percentages that define excellent achievement. Along with the drafts, an applicant should receive this explanation from the leader: "This is an employee partnering agreement draft for the job for which you are applying. It describes the areas of responsibility that the person in this job must take on in order to accomplish my expectations. It also lists the ways that I am committed to support the person in accomplishing my expectations. The expectations include excellent achievement statements that define the level of accomplishment that I expect for each expectation. During the interview, I will ask you to read each of the expectations out loud." The leader then asks the applicant, "Are you comfortable reading out loud?" The leader and the applicant discuss this issue if necessary.

The leader concludes the explanation by saying, "I will ask for your interpretation of each expectation and what you think it will take for you to accomplish each one at the desired level. Your answers to this last question will have the most influence on my rating of your capability to accomplish this job." The leader also asks the applicant if he or she has other questions about the interview. The leader answers these questions, confirms the interview date and time, and lets the applicant know that the leader looks forward to the interview.

In the interview, the leader follows through by asking the applicant to read the description paragraphs and tell the leader the applicant's interpretation of them. When that step is complete, the leader asks the applicant to read each excellent achievement statement and describe what the applicant thinks it will take for him or her to accomplish it at the level indicated.

As the interviewer listens, he or she considers how eager, how capable, and how committed the applicant is to accomplish the expectations. The interviewer uses the rating guide on the back of each expectation and the 1 to 4 scale to rate his or her impression for each expectation. As before, 1 is very low, 2 is less than excellent but not bad, 3 is excellent, and 4 is exceptional. These ratings are recorded in the blanks, and an average is computed and recorded, just as it is in a performance review. The leader totals the ratings for all expectations and compares rating totals to rank applicants.

These are the advantages to using partnering agreement drafts as interviewing and hiring tools:

- Because applicants have had the opportunity to learn about the job by studying the draft, the interviewer spends less time explaining the job. Furthermore, applicants are "tested" when they show how much they understand about the job as a result of studying the draft.
- Instead of thirty or forty interview questions, interviewers need remember only two questions: "What is your interpretation of each expectation?" and, "What support will you need to accomplish these expectations at the suggested level of achievement?"
- Interviewers automatically focus on issues important to the jobs and to applicants' abilities to accomplish the jobs.
- Applicants can be easily compared because achievement expectations have a built-in rating system.
- Applicants' responses are simple to record and easy to interpret.
- New hires learn how to operate with partnering agreements before they are hired.
- All questions are valid, fair, and legal.

Employee partnering is a researched and proven system that can be used in any organization. Its payoffs are many: a win-win culture is created, leaders share power and have more influence and success, work nurtures people as well as compensates them, and employee productivity and customer satisfaction increase in proportion to employee job satisfaction. The system also supports all performance improvement programs and helps organizations retain their seasoned and most-valued employees. The trend in all businesses is toward quality, empowerment, participation, and so forth. Partnering with employees is a foundational method of getting ahead of competition in the areas of these trends. Organizations do not need many programs, just one system done well.

Appendix

Examples of Partnering Agreements in Action

The Appendix exhibits illustrate how simply, effectively, and fairly partnering procedures guide leaders and direct reports in pinpointing and documenting the causes of low achievement. Those same advantages apply to partnering performance improvement plans, which address both leader and direct report shortcomings.

The exhibits show the minimal documentation needed to support leader-direct-report discussions and decisions on the causes of low achievement and on the remedies for these causes. There is one example for each of the four basic causes of low employee achievement. The documentation in each example is only a few notes, yet because it is set down in the context of a partnering agreement, it is sufficient to support extraordinarily effective procedures that generate continuous improvement in leadership and production activities. The prepared forms used for this partnering activity are the Low-Achievement Cause Checklist and the Low-Achievement Remedies Checklist. Because these forms remain the same, abbreviated versions of them are shown after the first examples.

The partnering process assures that employees understand what is expected of them and that they have appropriate support to achieve their commitments. The process also assures that employees help decide what it will take for them to resolve achievement shortcomings and maximizes the chances that employees will be ideally productive.

Cause One: Lack of Understanding or Support

A paralegal in a law office did not clearly understand the partners' expectations of her. Although the attorneys were not happy with Cele's performance, rather than talk to her about their dissatisfaction, they gave her bonuses and perks hoping these presumed "motivators" would cause her to accomplish more of the things they desired. However, Cele interpreted the bonuses and perks as evidence that she was doing fine, and the partners discovered that the bonuses and perks made matters worse not better. They also learned that they had to clarify and agree on their expectations before they could communicate the expectations to Cele.

The Low-Achievement Cause Checklist (Exhibit A.1) shows the conclusions of the discussions between Cele and the partners about the cause of Cele's low achievement. The notes in the left margin show that *all* the potential causes were discussed. The Low-Achievement Remedies Checklist (Exhibit A.2) describes the negotiated remedies that came out of the discussions.

Cause Two: Lack of Knowledge or Skill

One leadership expectation for a private club membership director stated she would supervise the club receptionist and a membership department assistant. The assistant's job did not pay much, but it was critical to the membership operation. The director, Cheryl, had had three assistants quit the job in the previous six months and was concerned about keeping the current one, Chris.

One of Chris's responsibilities was to help the receptionist hang coats during busy lunch hours. Chris worked in several locations in the office in order to be near machines and files necessary to her job. One location had one-way glass through which Chris could observe when the receptionist needed help hanging coats. Cheryl had asked Chris always to work at that location between 11:30 A.M. and 12:30 P.M. on busy days, so she could tell when her help was needed.

Chris did not like the receptionist and did not like to hang coats. She did everything she could to avoid the task. Cheryl was always exceptionally nice to everyone and refused to be controlling, and she did not know how to negotiate Chris's commitment to hanging coats without being controlling.

As a result, Chris rarely hung coats unless Cheryl asked her to do it. To keep from angering Chris, Cheryl often did not ask her, even when the job needed doing. In effect, Chris controlled Cheryl. The problem caused irritation among all office staff. The way Kevin, the club manager, discussed and resolved the situation with Cheryl is shown in Exhibits A.3 and A.4.

Cause Three: Lack of Capability

A company had reduced its workforce, and one of two accounts receivable clerks was terminated. Raymond, the remaining clerk, was told he would now have to call past due accounts to demand payment. During Raymond's achievement review, his leader, Adele, discovered that calling to demand payments bothered Raymond so much that he was physically unable to come to work on the designated calling days.

The documentation in Exhibit A.5 shows that Adele believed that Raymond's attitude and performance were so good in other areas of his job that he would no longer have to do that calling. She offered (Exhibit A.6) to assign the calling responsibility to someone else. That way Raymond could concentrate on important activities that he was good at and liked to do.

Cause Four: Lack of Commitment

Exhibits A.7 through A.12 illustrate a three-step personnel action that results in the termination of Sandy, a shop employee, for knowingly and repeatedly breaking safety rules. The exhibits show the discussion results and the actions taken: official warning, probation, and termination. Pat, Sandy's leader, gave him the warning after Sandy was observed using a "warning posted" grinder several times without wearing protective goggles. After Pat and Sandy discussed the incidents, Pat documented his decision and the action taken. Sandy cosigned the sheet with Pat to confirm that he understood and accepted the conclusion (Exhibits A.7 and A.8).

In the second episode (Exhibits A.9 and A.10) Sandy had been playing with a compressed-air hose and blew a metal shaving into another employee's eye. That resulted in another discussion with Pat. They documented the second discussion in the same way as the first, but the action defined was to put Sandy on official probation for safety policy violations. Pat explained to Sandy that another safety violation while Sandy was on probation was grounds for termination. Again, both Pat and Sandy signed the document.

Exhibits A.11 and A.12 document a third discussion between Pat and Sandy. Sandy was hit on the head by a bolt because he was not wearing his hard hat in a posted hard hat area. The action documented on the remedies checklist is termination.

This very simple discussion and documentation process assures that employees understand what is expected of them and that they have appropriate support to achieve expectations. In this example, the process shows that Sandy refused to accomplish what he committed to do. In effect, he terminated himself.

The partnering process maximizes employee's abilities to be ideally productive. It ensures that employees help decide what it will take for them to resolve their lack of commitment. Partnering agreements and reviews make the administrative work in addressing critical incidents simple and straightforward. The procedures also minimize the risk of successful litigation against employers by disgruntled employees.

Exhibit A.1. Low-Achievement Checklist: Cause One.

Leader *Parker Randolph* Title *Partner* Date *1-11-93*
Direct Report *Cele Schief* Title *Paralegal*
Review is for: Regular achievement review *X* Critical incident ___
Expectation under review: *Communication*
Situation summary: *The partners are disturbed that Cele's performance is disappointing. Without requests from her, we have given her bonuses, extra time off, new equipment, to improve her performance. We have not noticed any resulting positive change.*

Leader, study the checklist in relation to direct report's achievement of the expectation. Discuss each cause in sequence with direct report, to agree which one (or more) applies to the less-than-excellent achievement of the expectation.

Cause one: not sufficiently informed of expectations or not sufficiently supported.

1. Written company policy does not exist for, or does not adequately specify, the achievement expectation, so that direct report can accomplish it. *(agreed problem)*
2. Appropriate policy and performance standards exist but have not been formally discussed with direct report.
3. Sufficient information to accomplish this expectation has not been given to direct report. *(agreed problem)*
4. Existing company or leader practices inhibit direct report from accomplishing this expectation. *(agreed problem)*
5. Resources such as lead time, material, equipment, other people, procedures, decisions, and so forth that are beyond direct report's control were insufficient for direct report to accomplish this expectation. *(agreed circled items are problems)*

Cause two: not sufficiently trained. Direct report does not have sufficient knowledge or skill to accomplish this expectation.

Cause three: not sufficiently capable. Direct report has a mental or physical limitation that prevents him or her from having the potential to learn to accomplish this expectation.

Cause four: not sufficiently committed. . . .

Exhibit A.2. Low-Achievement Remedies Checklist: Cause One.

Leader, remedies are provided for each low-achievement cause. Once you and the direct report agree on the appropriate cause, select the corresponding remedy. Use it as a guide to prepare a plan to improve achievement of the expectation.

Remedy for cause one: not sufficiently informed or supported.

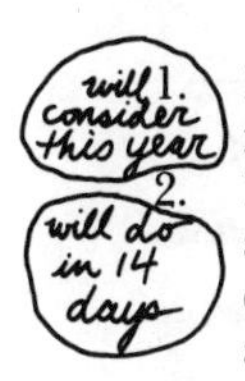

1. Prepare a company policy manual for all major operations. As a more immediate response, prepare a set of written policies that support direct report's job expectations.
2. Negotiate a partnering agreement with direct report that includes the excellent achievement of this expectation. During negotiation of the partnering agreement, discuss the following:
   a. Company policy related to this expectation.
   b. Inhibiting practices. Negotiate support and/or change in the inhibiting practices.
   c. Negotiate a plan to provide adequate support and resources or to change the achievement expectations.

will look at during evaluation

Remedy for cause two: not sufficiently trained. Select relevant training for direct report.

Remedy for cause three: not sufficiently capable. Reevaluate direct report and the expectation in order to change achievement expectations or recommend personnel position changes.

Remedy for cause four: not sufficiently committed. . . .

Summary of the action plan mutually worked out to improve performance of the expectation, or summary of the decision that will lead to termination: The partners will agree on and document our expectations as the basis for the draft of a team partnering agreement with Cele. I will negotiate the agreement with her when the partners have agreed on the draft. I will negotiate win-win resolutions with Cele on any other concerns that might surface while she and I are negotiating the agreement.

Parker Randolph 1-11-93

Exhibit A.3. Low-Achievement Checklist: Cause Two

Leader *Kevin Gross* Title *Club Manager* Date *8-13-92*
Direct Report *Cheryl Flaxton* Title *membership Director*
Review is for: Regular achievement review *X* Critical incident ____
Expectation under review: *Guiding employee performance improvement*
Situation summary: *Chris, Cheryl's assistant, does not like to do one of her assigned jobs, of helping the receptionist hang member and guest coats at lunchtime, 11:30 a.m. to 12:30 p.m. Cheryl continues to plead with Chris to do the job on her own when needed, but Chris does it only when asked.*

Leader, study the checklist in relation to direct report's achievement of the expectation. Discuss each cause in sequence with direct report, to agree which one (or more) applies to the expectation.

Cause one: not sufficiently informed of expectations or not sufficiently supported. . . .

agreed problem **Cause two:** not sufficiently trained. Direct report does not have sufficient knowledge or skill to accomplish this expectation.

Cause three: not sufficiently capable. Direct report has a mental or physical limitation that prevents him or her from having the potential to learn to accomplish this expectation.

Cause four: not sufficiently committed. . . .

Exhibit A.4. Low-Achievement Remedies Checklist: Cause Two.

Leader, remedies are provided for each low-achievement cause. Once you and the direct report agree on the appropriate cause, select the corresponding remedy. Use it as a guide to prepare a plan for improving achievement of the expectation.

Remedy for cause one: not sufficiently informed or supported. . . .

This is the remedy **Remedy for cause two:** not sufficiently trained. Select relevant training for direct report.

Remedy for cause three: not sufficiently capable. Reevaluate direct report and the expectation in order to change achievement expectations or recommend personnel position changes.

Remedy for cause four: not sufficiently committed. . . .

Summary of the action plan mutually worked out to improve performance of the expectation, or summary of the decision that will lead to termination: *Cheryl will learn that she must influence employees to be responsible for their actions and not continue to carry that responsibility herself. I will help Cheryl negotiate a commitment to this task with Chris. Cheryl will take training to learn how to negotiate employee commitment to expectations. I will help Cheryl to perfect this skill.* *Kevin Gross 8-13-92*

Exhibit A.5. Low-Achievement Checklist: Cause Three.

Leader *Adele Anderson* Title *Controller* Date *11-13-92*
Direct Report *Raymond Booton* Title *Accounts Receivable Clerk*
Review is for: Regular achievement review *X* Critical incident ____
Expectation under review: *Calling for overdue payments*
Situation summary: *Raymond survived a reduction in force in accounts receivable. Calling to demand payment for overdue accounts was added to his responsibilities. After three months, he started becoming too ill to work on days he was to call. The trauma affected all of his work.*

Leader, study the checklist in relation to direct report's achievement of the expectation. Discuss each cause in sequence with direct report, to agree which one (or more) applies to the expectation.

Cause one: not sufficiently informed of expectations or not sufficiently supported. . . .

Cause two: not sufficiently trained. Direct report does not have sufficient knowledge or skill to accomplish this expectation.

(agreed problem) **Cause three:** not sufficiently capable. Direct report has a mental or physical limitation that prevents him or her from having the potential to learn to accomplish this expectation.

Cause four: not sufficiently committed. . . .

Exhibit A.6. Low-Achievement Remedies Checklist: Cause Three.

Leader, remedies are provided for each low-achievement cause. Once you and your direct report agree on the appropriate cause, select the corresponding remedy. Use it as a guide to prepare a plan to improve achievement of the expectation.

Remedy for cause one: not sufficiently informed or supported. . . .

Remedy for cause two: not sufficiently trained. Select relevant training for direct report.

(agreed remedy) **Remedy for cause three:** not sufficiently capable. Reevaluate direct report and the expectation in order to change achievement expectations or recommend personnel position changes.

Remedy for cause four: not sufficiently committed. . . .

Summary of the action plan mutually worked out to improve performance of the expectation, or summary of the decision that will lead to termination: *I have agreed to remove this calling responsibility from Raymond's job. I do not believe any kind of training would help him. The rest of what Raymond does is too important to allow this activity to diminish his health and the balance of his performance.*

Adele Anderson 11-13-92

Exhibit A.7. Low-Achievement Checklist: Cause Four, Episode One.

Leader *Pat* Title *Supervisor* Date *10-17-92*
Direct Report *Sandy* Title *Production Worker*
Review is for: Regular achievement review ___ Critical incident *X*
Expectation under review: *safety and housekeeping*
Situation summary: *I observed Sandy using a grinder without wearing protective goggles. The machine was properly posted and Sandy had been warned previously for the same thing.*

Leader, study the checklist in relation to direct report's achievement of the expectation. Discuss each cause in sequence with direct report, to agree which one (or more) applies to the expectation.

Cause one: not sufficiently informed of expectations or not sufficiently supported. . . .

Cause two: not sufficiently trained. Direct report does not have sufficient knowledge or skill to accomplish this expectation.

Cause three: not sufficiently capable. Direct report has a mental or physical limitation that prevents him or her from having the potential to learn to accomplish this expectation.

(agreed cause) **Cause four:** not sufficiently committed. . . .

1. Direct report is not convinced this expectation is important enough to accomplish it as expected and allows other things to distract from achievement of this expectation.

Exhibit A.8. Low-Achievement Remedies Checklist: Cause Four, Episode One.

Leader, remedies are provided for each low-achievement cause. Once you and direct report agree on the appropriate cause, select the corresponding remedy. Use it as a guide to prepare a plan for improving achievement of the expectation.

Remedy for cause one: not sufficiently informed or supported. . . .

Remedy for cause two: not sufficiently trained. Select relevant training for direct report.

Remedy for cause three: not sufficiently capable. Reevaluate direct report and the expectation in order to change achievement expectations or recommend personnel position changes.

(agreed remedy) **Remedy for cause four:** not sufficiently committed. . . .

Summary of the action plan mutually worked out to improve performance of the expectation, or summary of the decision that will lead to termination: *Sandy agreed that he knew goggles were to be worn always when using that grinder. Sandy agreed to wear safety goggles as per policy. this is an official warning for Sandy. Pat Dirks 10-17-92*

I understand the warning. Sandy Jenkins 10-17-92

Exhibit A.9. Low-Achievement Checklist: Cause Four, Episode Two.

Leader *Pat* Title *Supervisor* Date *3-15-93*
Direct Report *Sandy* Title *Production worker*
Review is for: Regular achievement review ___ Critical incident *X*
Expectation under review: *Safety and housekeeping*
Situation summary: *Another employee was hurt when Sandy was horsing around with a compressed-air hose. It blew a metal sliver into the other person's eye.*

Leader, study the checklist in relation to direct report's achievement of the expectation. Discuss each cause in sequence with direct report, to agree which one (or more) applies to the expectation.

Cause one: not sufficiently informed of expectations or not sufficiently supported. . . .

Cause two: not sufficiently trained. Direct report does not have sufficient knowledge or skill to accomplish this expectation.

Cause three: not sufficiently capable. Direct report has a mental or physical limitation that prevents him or her from having the potential to learn to accomplish this expectation.

agreed cause → **Cause four:** not sufficiently committed. . . .

1. Direct report is not convinced this expectation is important enough to accomplish it as expected and allows other things to distract from achievement of this expectation.

Exhibit A.10. Low-Achievement Remedies Checklist: Cause Four, Episode Two.

Leader, remedies are provided for each low-achievement cause. Once you and direct report agree on the appropriate cause, select the corresponding remedy. Use it as a guide to prepare a plan for improving achievement of the expectation.

Remedy for cause one: not sufficiently informed or supported. . . .

Remedy for cause two: not sufficiently trained. Select relevant training for direct report.

Remedy for cause three: not sufficiently capable. Reevaluate direct report and the expectation in order to change achievement expectations or recommend personnel position changes.

agreed remedy **Remedy for cause four:** not sufficiently committed. . . .

Summary of the action plan mutually worked out to improve performance of the expectation, or summary of the decision that will lead to termination: *Sandy agreed that the injury happened without any thought because Sandy was horsing around with a live air hose. He agreed that he knew that was against company policy. Sandy is on probation for six months for safety.* *Pat Dirks 3-15-93*

I understand the probation. Sandy Jenkins 3-15-93

Exhibit A.11. Low-Achievement Checklist: Cause Four, Episode Three.

Leader Pat Title Supervisor Date 4-16-93

Direct Report Sandy Title Production Worker

Review is for: Regular achievement review ___ Critical incident X

Expectation under review: safety and housekeeping

Situation summary: Sandy was working in a posted hardhat area without his hardhat on. He was hit on the head by a bolt. He agreed that he knew he was supposed to wear his hard hat in that area.

Leader, study the checklist in relation to direct report's achievement of the expectation. Discuss each cause in sequence with direct report, to agree which one (or more) applies to the expectation.

Cause one: not sufficiently informed of expectations or not sufficiently supported. . . .

Cause two: not sufficiently trained. Direct report does not have sufficient knowledge or skill to accomplish this expectation.

Cause three: not sufficiently capable. Direct report has a mental or physical limitation that prevents him or her from having the potential to learn to accomplish this expectation.

(agreed cause) **Cause four:** not sufficiently committed. . . .

1. Direct report is not convinced this expectation is important enough to accomplish it as expected and allows other things to distract from achievement of this expectation.

Exhibit A.12. Low-Achievement Remedies Checklist: Cause Four, Episode Three.

Leader, remedies are provided for each low-achievement cause. Once you and direct report agree on the appropriate cause, select the corresponding remedy. Use it as a guide to prepare a plan for improving achievement of the expectation.

Remedy for cause one: not sufficiently informed or supported. . . .

Remedy for cause two: Not sufficiently trained. Select relevant training for direct report.

Remedy for cause three: Not sufficiently capable. Reevaluate direct report and the expectation in order to change achievement expectations or recommend personnel position changes.

(agreed remedy) **Remedy for cause four:** Not sufficiently committed. . . .

Summary of the action plan mutually worked out to improve performance of the expectation, or summary of the decision that will lead to termination: I explained that this was a violation of safety during his probation for safety. Per company policy, this is grounds for termination. Sandy's actions resulted in termination.

Pat Dirks 4-16-93

REFERENCES

Barker, J. *Discovering The Future: The Business Of Paradigms.* Minneapolis, Minn: Charthouse Learning Corporation, 1989. Videotape.

Block, P. *The Empowered Manager: Positive Political Skills at Work.* San Francisco: Jossey-Bass, 1987.

Coonradt, C., and Nelson, L. *The Game Of Work.* Salt Lake City, Utah: Shadow Mountain, 1985.

Covey, S. R. *The Seven Habits of Highly Effective People.* New York: Simon & Schuster, 1989.

Crosby, P. *Quality Without Tears.* New York: McGraw-Hill, 1984.

Deming, W. E. *Out of the Crisis.* Cambridge, Mass.: MIT CAES, 1986.

Drucker, P. *The New Realities.* New York: HarperCollins, 1989.

Graduate School of Agriculture. *Human Relations and Motivation.* Washington, D.C.: Graduate School, U.S. Department of Agriculture, 1971.

Herzberg, F. "One More Time: How Do You Motivate Employees?" *Harvard Business Review,* 1968, *46*(1), 26–35.

Juran, J. *Managerial Breakthrough.* New York: Fawcett, 1964.

Kopelman, R. E. "Improving Productivity Through Objective Feedback: A Review of the Evidence." *National Productivity,* 1983, *2*(1), 43–54.

Kouzes, J. M., and Posner, B. Z. *The Leadership Challenge: How to Get Extraordinary Things Done in Organizations.* San Francisco: Jossey-Bass, 1987.

Maslow, A. *Toward a Psychology of Being.* New York: Van Nostrand Reinhold, 1968.

Miller, L. *American Spirit.* New York: Warner, 1984.

Peale, N. V. *The Power of Positive Thinking.* Englewood Cliffs: Prentice-Hall, 1987.

Peale, N. V. *The Power of Positive Living.* New York: Doubleday, 1990.

Peters, T. *Thriving on Chaos.* New York: HarperCollins, 1987.

Peters, T., and Waterman, R. H., Jr. *In Search of Excellence.* New York: HarperCollins, 1982.

Platt, R. "Ego and Self-Actualization Needs as Productivity Incentives for Construction Craftsmen." Masters thesis, Colorado State University, 1979.

Senge, P. M. *The Fifth Discipline.* New York: Doubleday, 1990.

Walton, M. *The Deming Management Method.* New York: Putnam, 1986.

INDEX

J

K

L

M

N

O

P

R

S

T